The Denver Catholic Biblical School Program

SECOND YEAR

NEW TESTAMENT FOUNDATIONS: JESUS AND DISCIPLESHIP

STUDENT WORKBOOK

PAULIST PRESS

New York / Mahwah

Acknowledgments

The Publisher gratefully acknowledges use of the following materials: Excerpts from "Preaching to Corinthians," by Fred B. Craddock, copyright © April 1990, *Interpretation,* volume 44; excerpts from "Spokesmen for God," by Joseph Jensen, *God's Word to Israel,* copyright © 1984, Liturgical Press, Collegeville, MN; excerpts from "Outline of Psalms According to Literary Form," by Carroll Stuhlmueller, *Psalms I (Psalms 1–72)* in *Old Testament Message Series,* copyright © 1983, The Liturgical Press, Collegeville, MN; text and drawings as appeared in *The Bible Today,* January, 1984 excerpted from *St. Paul's Corinth,* by Jerome Murphy-O'Connor, copyright © 1983, The Liturgical Press, Collegeville, MN; "Catholic Update" articles appearing in this book were originally published by St. Anthony Messenger Press, Cincinnati, Ohio; excerpts from "How to Get to the Heart of a Pauline Letter," *Seven Pauline Letters,* by Peter F. Ellis, copyright © 1982, The Liturgical Press, Collegeville, MN, reprinted with permission; excerpts from *Community of the Beloved Disciple,* by Raymond Brown, copyright © 1979, Paulist Press, Mahwah, NJ.

"Special thanks are given to Mary Ingenthron for the biblical drawings that are included throughout this book."

Censor Deputatus:
  Jean-Pierre Ruiz, S.T.D.

Nihil Obstat:
  J. Anthony McDaid, J.C.D.

Imprimatur:
  ✠ J. Francis Stafford
  Archbishop of Denver
  Denver, November 28, 1994

The Imprimatur is an official declaration that a book or pamphlet is free of doctrinal or moral error. No implication is contained therein that those who have granted the Imprimatur agree with the contents, opinions or statements expressed.

ISBN: 0-8091-9421-X

Published by Paulist Press
997 Macarthur Boulevard
Mahwah, NJ 07430

Printed and bound in the United States of America

CONTENTS

Supplementary Readings

Foreword

This book is the fruit of ten years of collaborative work in the Archdiocese of Denver. Archbishop James V. Casey of happy memory had a vision of a serious program of biblical study which would meet the needs and utilize the leadership potential of the many Catholics leaving the Catholic Church to attend fundamentalist Bible Colleges. He established the Catholic Biblical School in 1982. After his death it would expand greatly thanks to the support of Archbishop J. Francis Stafford.

Archbishop Casey entrusted the carrying out of his vision to me, and in time I was joined by teachers of outstanding competence and dedication: Steve Mueller, Ph.D., Angeline Hubert, Gene Giuliano, Dorothy Jonaitis, O.P., Kim Barta, and Kathy McGovern. Each contributed unique gifts to the development of the program.

We also received excellent organizational and clerical help from Tina Gargan, Audrey Jonas, Carol Perito, and Helen Williams. Without their support the cohesive program we have developed would have fallen apart at many places.

The most important collaborators of all have been our students—about 2,000 of them, each bringing a unique eagerness for the word of God and insight into it. Every detail of this program has been evaluated by them year after year and revised in the light of their experience.

Among the students who have been part of us from the very beginning, Mary Ingenthron has gifted us in a very special way with her creative talents. The illustrations in this book are among her many contributions.

We have also been blessed by the supervision of two Archdiocesan Directors of Catholic Education, Reverend Joseph M. O'Malley and Very Reverend J. Anthony McDaid, and the enthusiastic support of the priests and staff members of the archdiocese.

Through all of our shared work it has been evident that what has happened among us has been far beyond our combined ability; the Catholic Biblical School has been truly the work of the Spirit of God. It is our prayer that through this book this work of the Spirit may spread wherever people are hungry for God's word.

It is our hope that those who use these books will be able to share their experience, support one another in the work of biblical education, and be able to offer programs with similar structure and requirements so that students could transfer without difficulty. If you are interested in becoming part of this Catholic Biblical School network and wish to receive our newsletter *Connections,* please contact The Catholic Biblical School of the Archdiocese of Denver, 200 Josephine Street, Denver, CO 80206 [(303) 388-4411].

Macrina Scott, O.S.F.

Student's Introduction

Welcome to the second year of your journey of Bible study! You are now a seasoned traveler after your journey with Abraham, Moses, Joshua, David and Solomon. Your study has provided you with a good grasp of the story of God's power and presence with the Hebrew people. You must continue to keep this Old Testament foundation in mind this year as you explore the fulfillment of the Old Testament in Jesus Christ. In this second year we concentrate on the amazing story of God's presence among us in the person and work of Jesus of Nazareth, and the impact this had on early Christian apostles like Peter and Paul, the evangelists Mark, Luke and John, and John the author of the Book of Revelation.

A Preview of the Second Year Journey

In the first unit, we study the written gospels of Mark and Luke. In these writings we meet Jesus and hear his message. We follow his journey from Nazareth throughout Galilee to Jerusalem. Through his passion and death and resurrection we are confronted with the central mystery of our Christian faith.

In the second unit, we follow the growth of the Christian community as it is recounted in Luke's Acts of the Apostles. Focusing on the journeys of Peter and Paul, Luke reveals the guiding hand of God working together with these apostles for the spread of the Christian message.

During this unit we also study most of the letters of Paul. These are the earliest documents of our Christian heritage. Paul's missionary endeavors also demanded that he start and guide the fledgling Christian communities through the challenging process of turning from their pagan or Jewish practices and learning to do things in the Christian way. His letters open a window for us into the practicalities of living a Christian life in a world which as yet had been unaffected by the ideas and values of Christianity. Paul's concerns are surprisingly similar to the kinds of challenges that we still face today as we try to live out our Christian lives.

In the third unit, we study two books which are very different. Familiar as we might be with the gospels of Mark and Luke from the first unit, we discover that John's gospel is very different from these. Can you imagine a gospel in which Jesus does not teach in parables and performs only a few miracles (none of which is a driving out of evil spirits!)?

We also enter into the strange world of the Book of Revelation. Almost everyone who tries to read this book is perplexed by the strange and apparently bizarre imagery in which the author presents the Christian message. But through our careful study, we can begin to understand the meaning of this book and how it still has a message for us today.

Thus our second year will be a journey to the center of our Christian faith. We will deal with the many ways that the Christian message is presented to us — in the narratives of gospels of Mark, Luke-Acts, and John, in the problem-solving letters of Paul to his Christian communities, and in the imaginative visions of the Book of Revelation. We will discover that beneath this variety of forms, the core Christian message is the same — our salvation comes through the life, death and resurrection of Jesus who is indeed the Christ sent by God.

Preparing for the Second Year Journey

One of the most important things for you to do as you prepare for this year is to reread the Vatican II *Dogmatic Constitution on Divine Revelation (Dei*

Verbum) to review again the guidelines for the approach to scripture recommended by the Catholic Church. Since we never adequately interpret the meaning of scripture without taking into account our tradition and the liturgical use of scripture in our believing and celebrating Church, we need to reflect constantly on the way in which the Church guides our approach to these texts.

As you learned last year, you need a good translation of the Bible for your study. We recommend that you use the revised New Testament translation found in the *New American Bible* (1986) which was commissioned by the U. S. Catholic Bishops. This revision is completely redone and much more adequate than the previous 1970 translation. The notes have been expanded and are very helpful for students who are trying to understand the text. The best edition of this translation comes in the *Oxford Catholic Study Bible* or the *Catholic Student Bible,* which both contain articles and study guides for the student.

Other translations which are also suitable are the *Revised Standard Version* (RSV) or *New Revised Standard Version* (NRSV), or *The New Jerusalem Bible* (NJB). Reading more than one translation is an excellent way of discovering new meanings in texts that might have become all too familiar from hearing them in church.

As always, your McKenzie *Dictionary of the Bible* is a treasure chest of background materials which will help the biblical texts come alive. Your Hammond *Atlas of the Bible Lands* will help you become familiar with the places of the world of Jesus and Paul. You might also want to investigate other Bible atlases which give even more lavish pictures and maps that can help you put pictures with the words of scripture so that the events really come alive for you as you study.

For each unit of study, we will also recommend textbooks that we have found helpful for understanding this New Testament material. In particular, Pheme Perkins' *Reading the New Testament* will help you begin to find your way through this year of studies. There has been a great increase in the number of helpful books about the New Testament in the last fifteen years. You should check what is available through your public library or other libraries to which you have access. Your teacher can also suggest further books which you might find helpful with the topics which begin to spark your interest.

Making the Journey

You are now already familiar with the process of making the biblical journey using our study materials. The assignment questions lead you directly to the Bible texts which you have been assigned to read. One thing that you will notice is that this year the number of biblical chapters is often less than last year. But don't let the number fool you. A new depth of study is required for the New Testament material. Since you are reading and studying for more than mere information, your involvement with this material will be stimulating changes in your thinking and your actions.

Each week we also provide "optional challenges" which require a bit more thinking and research than our basic questions. Of course, you will certainly find many other intriguing things which you might like to follow up on as you study. Make these into optional challenges and share them with your group.

You will also have a question for which you do not have to write out an answer but which you are expected to think about so that you can discuss it with your small group. Many of these questions relate to the comparison of texts from the gospels in order to discover the reasons why Luke or Matthew might have changed Mark's text. These questions will challenge your ability to compare texts and to reflect on the reasons for their differences.

We also suggest a memory verse for each lesson. Sometimes you might think that memorizing these and other verses of scripture is irrelevant. But these verses are the first step in making the

Bible texts your own. Without some memorization, it is difficult to have scripture texts readily available for your prayer and application to the situations of your life.

Companions for Your Journey

As you learned throughout your previous year, some of your best teachers are the people from your small group with whom you shared your journey. Again this year, these pilgrimage companions will surprise you with their insights about Jesus and his message. Just as the evangelists Mark, Luke, and John, the apostle Paul, and John the author of the Book of Revelation can each take a special perspective on who Jesus is and what he means for them and their communities, so each one in your group will have his or her special viewpoint on the material you study each week. Listening to God's word occurs not just as it is encapsulated in the scripture text, but also as it is incarnated in the persons with whom you study.

As before, your group sharing should be guided by

The Ten Commandments of Group Process

1. Work to build trust and intimacy within your group.

2. Get to the heart of the passage.
   Don't just skim the surface.

3. Give everyone in your group a chance to talk.
   No speeches!

4. Speak connectedly with previous speakers.
   Consciously work at building bridges with what has already been said.

5. While one person speaks, everyone else listens.

6. Never ridicule or cut down another's answers.

7. When you disagree, do so with respect.

8. Do not fear silence.

9. If you have not done your homework, answer only the questions which your instructor designates.

10. Enjoy yourself!

As always, the journey brings many surprises. You might be beginning your New Testament study by thinking that you know pretty much what the gospel is and what the message of the gospels is. After a few weeks of study, you might find out that what you thought you knew was not really well-known at all. The power and the mystery of the gospels always open our minds and hearts to new meanings. So, as Vatican II's *Dei Verbum* encourages, "through reading and study of the sacred books, let the Word of God run and be glorified (2 Thess 3:1) and let the treasure of revelation entrusted to the Church increasingly fill your hearts"(# 26).

Remember, as you work on God's Word, God's Word works on you!

HOW THE STORY OF JESUS GOT INTO THE GOSPELS

AN OVERVIEW OF YEAR TWO — UNIT ONE

Jesus: Two Synoptic Views

Objectives

1. To become familiar with the chronology, geography, and historical-social environment of New Testament Christianity.
2. To understand the Christian message in its narrative presentation (gospel) through an investigation of the structure, sources, themes and theologies of Mark and Luke.
3. To gain both familiarity and skill in the methods of literary-historical criticism, in particular form criticism and redaction criticism of the gospel text.
4. To increase your ability to use scripture for personal and communal prayer.

Textbooks

P. Perkins   *Reading the New Testament* (Revised Edition)
J. McKenzie   *Dictionary of the Bible* (MDB)
W. Kelber   *Mark's Story of Jesus*
K. Aland (ed.) *Synopsis of the Four Gospels*
Hammond's   *Atlas of Bible Lands*

Assignments

I.1   APPROACHING THE GOSPELS

I.2   MARK: Chapters 1–3

I.3   MARK: Chapters 4:1–8:21

I.4   MARK: Chapters 8:22–12:44

I.5   MARK: Chapters 14–16

I.6   INFANCY NARRATIVES: Luke 1–2; Matthew 1–2

I.7   LUKE: Chapters 3:1–9:50

I.8   LUKE: Chapters 9:51–19:27

I.9   LUKE: Chapters 19:28–20:47; 22–24

I.10   UNIT REVIEW AND EXAM

I.1: Approaching the Gospels

Read: "Instruction of the Pontifical Biblical Commission on the Historical Truth of the Gospels," # 1, and "The Three Stages of the Composition of the Gospels (Vatican II)," # 2 in your SUPPLEMENTARY READINGS found at the end of this book, pp. 63, 68; MDB: History and Historical Writing, Interpretation, Inspiration; Perkins pp. 1-21.

Geography Task   On the map on page 24 of your Hammond *Atlas of the Bible Lands,* locate the Roman provinces of Syria, Galatia, Asia, Macedonia and the Kingdom of Herod. In the Kingdom of Herod, locate the Sea of Galilee, the Jordan River, the Dead Sea, Judea and Samaria.

p.363

1. Based on your reading of the MDB article on History and Historical Writing, please describe in your own words Israel's concept of "history."

2. In your own words, please list and briefly explain the three stages of gospel formation.

3. Based on your reading of these two articles, please give your description of what a written gospel is. (*Hint:* Be sure to include ideas concerning the evangelist's purpose, audience, historical situation, etc.)

4. Share some incident from your past or your family's past where understanding the "meaning" of the event has proved to be more important than remembering the exact details of the incident.

5. What is the most important thing you have learned from your study of these readings?

> However, since God speaks in sacred Scripture through men in human fashion, the interpreter of sacred Scripture, in order to see clearly what God wanted to communicate to us, should carefully investigate what meaning the sacred writers really intended, and what God wanted to manifest by means of their words.
>
> — Vatican II, *Dogmatic Constitution on Divine Revelation (Dei Verbum)*, # 12

> Let the interpreters bear in mind that their foremost and greatest endeavor should be to discern and define clearly that sense of the biblical words which is called literal...so that the mind of the author may be made clear.
>
> — Pope Pius XII, *Divino Afflante Spiritu* (1943), # 23

SUGGESTIONS FOR THE STUDENT

After studying this lesson, you should:

1. Be able to explain the three stages of gospel formation: the development of gospel events to oral proclamation to written gospels. [See "The Three Stages of the Composition of the Gospels," # 2 in your SUPPLEMENTARY READINGS.]

2. Understand the key role of authors and their human contribution in this process.

3. Recognize that the same gospel content can be presented through many forms of presentation. [See "Truth and Its Many Expressions: Vatican II on How to Interpret the Scriptures, # 3 in your SUPPLEMENTARY READINGS.]

4. Know that the literary form of the gospels is that of a narrative proclamation of the good news of our Christian salvation.

5. Understand that in the gospels we are dealing with the Christian community's "faith" interpretation and application of the events concerning Jesus Christ and not simply a journalistic reporting of them.

Memory Verse Suggestion:

Mark 1:14-15 — "This is the time of fulfillment. The Kingdom of God is at hand. Reform your lives and believe in the good news."

I.2: Mark 1–3

Read: Mark 1–3; Kelber pp. 9-29; Perkins pp. 51-77; 203-213.

Geography Task   Using maps on p. 26 and p. 27 of your *Atlas*, locate: Galilee, Nazareth, Bethsaida, Capernaum, Gennesaret, Tyre, Sidon.

1. The answer to the question, "Who is Jesus?" is very important in the first half of this gospel.
   a) What do you learn from the testimonies and events of chapter 1 about the identity of Jesus?
   b) What do you discover about the identity of Jesus from the five "conflict" stories found in Mark 2:1-3:6?

2. What do you learn about what it means to be a disciple from the "call" stories of Mark 1:14-20 and 2:13-17?

3. Markan Themes: Understanding/Misunderstanding Jesus
   From Mark 1-3 briefly list who demonstrates a correct understanding of who Jesus is and who misunderstands who Jesus is. If a reason is given in the text for any misunderstanding, please make a note of it. For a fuller appreciation of the importance of this theme for Mark, continue to add to your list each week until you have traced this theme through the whole gospel. Hand in your completed work with Assignment I.5.

4. Jesus' first words in Mark are, "This is the time of fulfillment. The Kingdom of God is at hand! Reform your lives and believe in the gospel!" Which passage from Mark 1–3 speaks most to you of the Good News of the Kingdom of God? Why?

Small Group Exercise   Gospel Parallels (*Synopsis of the Four Gospels*)
(This does not have to be written out but must be prepared for your small group discussion. The small group facilitator for this class session will report on this exercise after the discussion.) For a method of procedure to use as "A Handy Guide to Using the *Gospel Parallels*," see # 5 in your SUPPLEMENTARY READINGS.
1. Locate Mark 1:41 and 3:5 in your *Synopsis of the Four Gospels*.
2. Note how Matthew and Luke change what Mark has written.
3. Why do you suppose the later evangelists might have wanted to change these references to Jesus' feelings? (Maybe Matthew 5:21-22 could give a clue!)

Optional Challenges
1. Compare and contrast [that is, tell what is similar and what is different in] the portrayal of Jesus and John the Baptist as found in these opening chapters. What do you learn from this?
2. In some art form (picture, poetry, reflection, prayer, etc.) portray the appearance of Jesus on the scene as described in Mark 1–3.
3. What do you think Mark is trying to tell his audience in the "harsh" story of Jesus' family in 3:20-21, 31-35? (In what way might this story reflect an experience that Mark's community might be familiar with?)

SUGGESTIONS FOR THE STUDENT

After studying this lesson, you should:

1. See that the gospels revolve around two major questions:
   1. Who is Jesus?
   2. What does it mean to be his disciple?

2. Be able to identify understanding / misunderstanding as a key Markan theme.

3. Understand the overall structure of Mark's gospel.

4. Understand the basic relationships of Mark to the other synoptic gospels. See "The Synoptic Sources and Comparisons," # 4 in your SUPPLEMENTARY READINGS.

Memory Verse Suggestion:

Mark 2:17 —   "Those who are well do not need a physician, but the sick do. I did not come to call the righteous, but sinners."

Other Exercises:

Following the footsteps of Jesus:
Draw or copy a map of the Holy Land. Then follow Jesus' "activities" and journeys on the map. You might want to use different colored pencils for each chapter or section of the gospel. This exercise is very interesting for the analysis of Mark, chapters 5–8. It is also interesting to compare if you do one for each of the gospels.

Mark 1:29-31   Simon's mother-in-law cured

I.3: Mark 4:1–8:21

Read: Mark 4:1–8:21; Kelber pp. 30-42; Perkins pp. 78-90.

Helpful topics in MDB: Elijah, Parable.

Geography   Using maps on p. 26 and p. 27 of your *Atlas*, locate: Gerasa, Decapolis.
Task

1. What do you think Jesus is attempting to teach about the Kingdom of God in the parables of Mark 4:26-32?

2. Mark 6:1-6, 14-16 speaks of some inaccurate or insufficient answers which were given to the question, "Who is Jesus?"
    a) Identify two of these insufficient answers.
    b) Are these same insufficient answers found in our world today?

3. Based on your reading of Mark 7, briefly explain the "new morality" Jesus teaches and how it differs from the morality taught by the Pharisees.

4. Markan Themes: Universality (i.e. the inclusiveness of all) in the Kingdom Jesus is building. List and briefly explain how any two passages from this week's gospel reading demonstrate this theme.

5. What is the most important thing you have learned about the Kingdom of God from these chapters from Mark?

6. Write a modern-day parable about the Kingdom of God. Begin it simply with the words "The Kingdom of God is like...
    (Before you write, recall what a parable is; why it is told; how it makes its point. Your answer to question #5 above may give you an idea of what you might want to say about the Kingdom of God in your parable. Do not *explain* your parable; let your reader do that!)

Small Group   Gospel Parallels Work
Exercise
1. Locate the passage Mark 4:35-41 in your *Synopsis of the Four Gospels*.
2. Note how Matthew and Luke change Mark.
3. Are Jesus and/or his disciples portrayed any differently because of these changes? If so, how?

Optional   1. What is the meaning of the parable of the sower (Mark 4:3-9) for you personally?
Challenges   (Please do not use the interpretation of Mark 4:14-20. Instead, explain how this parable applies to your own life.)
                  2. Express either the "Miracle Section" of Mark 4:35-5:43 or the "Bread Section" of Mark 6:31–8:21 in some artistic/literary form.

SUGGESTIONS FOR THE STUDENT

After studying this lesson, you should:

1. Understand the nature of parable — how it works and why it is appropriate for communicating the mystery of the Kingdom of God.

2. Be able to see how Jesus' moral teaching differs from that of the Pharisees as they are depicted in Mark's gospel.

3. Understand Mark's idea of the purpose and meaning of Jesus' miracles and the role they play in relation to the Kingdom of God.

Memory Verse Suggestion:

Mark 4:11 — "The mystery of the Kingdom of God has been given to you. But to those outside everything comes in parables...."

Other Exercises:

For Mark, the opposite of faith is fear. Read the gospel noting the times that Mark uses the words "faith" or "believe" and "fear" (awe). Reflect on how this contrast of "faith/fear" might give us a deeper insight today concerning our faith. Would it be more helpful to think as Mark does rather than in our usual categories of faith/unbelief? After doing this exercise you might compare your findings with the article "Faith and Fear in Mark's Gospel," *Bible Today*, vol. 23, no. 5, September 1985.

Mark 6:7 John the Baptist imprisoned

I.4: Mark 8:22–12:44

Read: Mark 8:22–12:44; Kelber pp. 43-70; Perkins Chapter 2, "The World of Jesus," pp. 23-50.

Helpful topics in MDB: Clean/Unclean, Cloud, Divorce, Gehenna, Hosanna, Lord, Love, Meals (Messianic Banquet), Messiah, Son of God, Son of Man, Theophany, Transfiguration.

Geography Task Using map on p. 28 in your *Atlas*, locate: Caesarea Philippi. On p. 29, locate: Bethphage; Jerusalem; Mount of Olives; Solomon's Porch; Golgotha.

1. The two miracle stories of 8:22-27 and 10:46-52 frame the "passion prediction"/ "journey" section in Mark and so comment on its meaning. How do these miracle stories alert us to what is happening on the way to Jerusalem?

2. Based on your reading of the passion predictions (8:31-38; 9:31-50; 10:32-45) and the subsequent interchanges between Jesus and his disciples, what do you see as Mark's understanding of:
   a) Who Jesus is?
   b) What it means to be his follower?

3. In Mark 11:12-25, Mark intercalates (i.e. frames one incident between two parts of another incident — a sandwich effect in order for the two incidents to explain each other) the cleansing of the temple between two parts of the cursing of the fig tree story. How do these two incidents symbolize the end of the Old Covenant?

4. In Mark 12:13-17 Jesus cleverly resolves the legal question of what is owed to Caesar, but he does not answer the question of what belongs to God. Based on what Jesus says and does in this story, what do you conclude belongs to God? (Note Genesis 1:27)

5. Imagine you are living during the time of Jesus and are writing a letter to your family in Jerusalem. Describe to your family your reaction to what Jesus has been saying and doing. (Reflect on material in the first twelve chapters of Mark.)

Small Group Exercise Gospel Parallels Work
1. Locate Mark 8:27-33 in your *Synopsis of the Four Gospels*.
2. Note how Matthew and Luke differ from Mark.
3. What might be the reason(s) for Matthew and Luke making their changes? (Especially note the changes Matthew makes.)

Optional Challenges 1. Express the "Journey Section" of Mark 8:31–10:52 in some art or prayer form.
2. Which passage from Mark 8:22–12:44 is most meaningful for you? Why?

SUGGESTIONS FOR THE STUDENT

After studying this lesson, you should:

1. Recognize the general form of a miracle story and of a pronouncement story. [See Perkins, pp. 52-58.]

2. Recognize the often used Markan technique of *intercalation* or framing.

3. Understand more concretely how Mark is organizing his gospel.

Memory Verse Suggestion:

Mark 8:34 —   "If any want to become my followers, let them deny themselves, take up their cross and follow me."

Mark 10:14-15 Jesus and the children

I.5: Mark 14–16

Read: Mark 14–16; Kelber pp. 71-96; Perkins pp. 91-97.

Helpful topics in MDB: Abba, Anoint, Bethany, Burial, Covenant (NT), Cross, Elders, Gabbatha, Gethsemane, Golgotha, King, Passion, Passover, Pilate, Priest (high), Rabbi, Sanhedrin.

Geography Task

On the map of Jerusalem, p. 29 in your *Atlas*, trace the events of Holy Week.

1. What does Mark's account of Jesus' anointing (14:3-9) reveal about the Messiah ("anointed one") which seems to reverse common expectation?

2. Markan Themes: Jesus' Relationship to God
   What does Jesus' prayer in Gethsemane (14:32-42) reveal about his own understanding of his relationship to God?

3. What details of Mark's passion story have been influenced by Psalm 22:1-22? Please give references.

4. If Mark were the only gospel version you had, what would be your personal reaction/response to the passion narrative and the "empty tomb" story of chapters 14:1–16:8 (Mark's original ending)?

5. Reflect on the entire gospel of Mark. Please describe your thoughts and feelings about this book.

6. Choose a memory verse from Mark's gospel (including chapter and verse and Bible translation used). Recite it for your small group and share with them why you chose this verse.

Small Group Exercise

Gospel Parallels Work
1. Locate Mark 14:56-65 in your *Synopsis of the Four Gospels.*
2. Note the charges brought against Jesus in Matthew and Luke.
3. Note Jesus' final answer in each version and how Luke's version is different.

Optional Challenges

1. How does Mark's original ending of 16:7-8 reaffirm his portrait of the disciples in his gospel version?
2. What is the significance of the absence of post-resurrection appearances by Jesus in Mark (16:9-20 is not Mark's work but a later addition)? What might this reveal about the situation of Mark's community?
3. Which passage from Mark 14–16 is most meaningful for you? Why?
4. How would our Christian lives be different if Mark were our only gospel?

SUGGESTIONS FOR THE STUDENT

After studying this lesson, you should:

1. Understand the meaning of "Messiah" from Mark's point of view and why this understanding of Jesus was relevant to the needs of his community.

2. Understand the structure of Mark's passion account. See # 6, "An Outline of Mark's Passion" in your SUPPLEMENTARY READINGS.

3. Understand how the New Testament writers (especially Mark) use the Old Testament as a source for interpreting the meaning of the passion event. [In particular: Suffering Servant, Psalm 22]

4. Be better acquainted with the geography of Jerusalem.

Memory Verse Suggestion:

Mark 15:39 — "When the centurion who stood facing him saw how he breathed his last he said, 'Truly this man was the Son of God.'"

Other Exercises:

- Trace the passion route on a map of your own.
- Review the basic information about Mark's gospel by using "The Gospel According to Mark: Overview," # 7 in your SUPPLEMENTARY READINGS.
- Do the Self-Quiz on Mark, # 15 in your SUPPLEMENTARY READINGS.

Mark 16:1   Women bring spices to the tomb

I.6: Infancy Narratives

Read: Matthew 1–2; Luke 1–2; Sr. Macrina Scott, "How To Read the Nativity Stories of Jesus," # 9 in your SUPPLEMENTARY READINGS.

Geography Task   Using map on p. 24 in your *Atlas*, locate: Egypt.
Using map on p. 25 in your *Atlas*, locate: Bethlehem, Nazareth.

1. Answer each of the following for Luke 1–2 *only:*
    A. To whom did God send a message about the birth of a child?
        Who was the messenger?
        What was the child named (or to be named)?
    B. Who comes to honor the new-born child?
        As far as you can tell, are they Jews or Gentiles? Rich or poor?
    C. What events occur in the temple?
    D. What Old Testament prophecies does the evangelist *say* are fulfilled?
    E. What women play a part in the story?
    F. Do you find these familiar Christmas images in these chapters?
        a. the star
        b. the angels singing "Glory to God in the highest"
        c. the manger
        d. the wise men's camels
        e. the ox and the ass
        f. the "three kings"
        g. the flight into Egypt
        h. the slaughter of children by Herod

2. Answer all of question #1 for Matthew 1–2 *only.*

3. Each infancy narrative goes *only* with the gospel in which it is found. How do the differences between the infancy narratives of Matthew and Luke illustrate the different emphases of each gospel? (Perhaps your answers to questions #1 and #2 above may help.)

4. Lukan Themes: Prayer
    Luke uses this theme more than any other evangelist. Identify passages from Luke 1–2 which deal with people praying (giving praise, etc.). Identify WHO PRAYS, the CONTENT of the prayer (i.e. simply summarize what is prayed for, if you can tell), and note any accompanying FEELINGS, POSTURES, SETTINGS, for the prayer. For a fuller appreciation of the importance of this theme for Luke, continue to add to your list each week until you have traced this theme through the whole gospel.

Optional Challenges   1. Express the "atmosphere" created by each infancy narrative in some prayer or art form (i.e. express the overall "feeling" and "attitude" as you perceive it in each version).
2. Depict each "Christmas" story in an art or prayer form.

SUGGESTIONS FOR THE STUDENT

After studying this lesson, you should:

1. Be able to distinguish between the Matthew and Luke infancy narratives and appreciate their uniqueness rather than collapsing both together. But see the chart on material that Luke and Matthew share, # 8 in your SUPPLEMENTARY READINGS.

2. See that the infancy narratives serve as overtures to the gospels and that in them can be found the evangelist's theology which will be developed throughout his gospel version. Each infancy narrative goes only with the gospel in which it is found.

3. Understand that the infancy narratives, like the gospels themselves, are not first historical but *theological* in their purpose.

4. Appreciate Matthew and Luke's dependence on the Old Testament in the development of their infancy materials. See "The Annunciation Pattern," # 10 in your SUPPLEMENTARY READINGS.

Memory Verse Suggestion:

Luke 2:11 —   "For today in the city of David a savior has been born for you who is Messiah and Lord."

Matthew 1:22-23 —   "All this took place to fulfill what the Lord had said through the prophet: Behold, the virgin shall be with child and bear a son, and they shall name him Emmanuel, which means 'God is with us.'"

I.7: Luke 3:1–9:50

Read: Luke 3:1–9:50; Perkins pp. 229-241.

Helpful topics in MDB: Beatitudes, Centurion, Fasting, Forgiveness, Genealogy, Gospel, Lamp, Luke, Spirit, Temptation.

Geography Task   Using maps on pp. 26-27 in your *Atlas*, locate: Iturea, Trachonitis, Abilene, Nain.

1.   Using your *Synopsis* book, compare Luke's account of the ministry of John the Baptist with that of Mark 1:2-8.
     a)   What do Luke's additions tell you about John and his mission?
     b)   How would Luke's presentation of John be more appealing to a predominantly Gentile audience?

2.   In 4:1-30,
     a)   List the passages in which Luke refers to the Old Testament either by direct quote or indirect allusion.
     b)   How do these references help to identify Jesus and his mission?

3.   In 5:1-11, Luke synthesizes the two "call" stories of Mark 1:16-20:
     a)   Of those called in Luke's account, who is prominent?
     b)   How is this person depicted?
     c)   What do you learn about discipleship from this "call" story?

4.   Briefly discuss what you think are the three most important characteristics of the new way of life as taught by Jesus in Luke 6:12–7:50.

5.   In Luke 9:9 Herod asks, "Who is this man about whom I hear all these reports?" How would you answer *based only on the material in Luke 9:9-50?*

6.   Lukan Themes: Table Fellowship or Banquet
     Luke often uses meal settings to teach lessons for his community. What do you learn from the meal stories of Luke 5:27-39 and 7:36-50 about:
     a)   who Jesus is?
     b)   those whom Jesus calls?

Small Group Exercise   Gospel Parallels Work
1.   Locate Luke 7:36-50 in your *Synopsis of the Four Gospels*.
2.   Compare Luke's anointing scene with that of Mark.
3.   Why would Luke locate this scene during Jesus' ministry rather than at the start of the passion as Mark has it?
     What changes does Luke make which reveal his emphasis on who Jesus is?
     What changes does Luke make in the other characters which reveal his emphasis on what the proper response to Jesus ought to be?

Optional Challenges   1.   Depict Luke 4:18-19 in some prayer or art form.
2.   In Luke 9:37-50 (the disciples' first mission), the evangelist may be indirectly reflecting a missionary problem which his own community has. Based on this passage:
     a)   What might the problem be?
     b)   What might the solution be?

SUGGESTIONS FOR THE STUDENT

After studying this lesson, you should:

1. Understand and apply the methods of redaction criticism to discover the evangelist's work as an editor. For a list of the special material which Luke used in addition to Mark and "Q," see "Passages Unique to Luke's Gospel — 'L' Passages," # 11 in your SUPPLEMENTARY READINGS.

2. Be able to identify the Lukan themes of: fulfillment, salvation history, Christian community as the "New Israel," discipleship, prayer, and Eucharist.

3. Understand Luke's particular emphasis concerning Jesus and discipleship.

Memory Verse Suggestion:

Luke 6:27 — "But to you who hear I say, love your enemies, do good to those who hate you, bless those who curse you, pray for those who mistreat you."

Luke 4:1-4   Not by bread alone

I.8: Luke 9:51–19:27

Read: Luke 9:51–19:27.

Helpful topics in MDB: Father, Jonah (NT), Lord's Prayer, Samaria, Samaritans, Sin.

Geography   Using map on p. 26 in your *Atlas*, locate: Chorazin. On p. 9, locate: Nineveh.
Task

1. What do you learn about the Christian manner of loving God and neighbor from Luke 10:25-42?

2. Luke summarizes much of his view of Christian prayer in 11:1-13. Based on your reading of this passage:
   a) Who is to pray the "Lord's Prayer," an individual or a community?
   b) Why ought one to pray?
   c) For what ought one to pray?
   d) How does Luke 11:13 differ from Matthew 7:11?

3. What do the three parables of Luke 15:3-32 have to say concerning the pastoral problem of reconciliation of sinners within the community?

4. Lukan Themes: The Right Use of Wealth
   Please summarize what is taught concerning this theme in 16:1-31.

5. Which passage from this "Journey Section" in Luke do you find most meaningful for your own journey to God?

Small Group   Gospel Parallels Work
Exercise
1. Locate Luke 18:35-43 in your *Synopsis of the Four Gospels*.
2. Note Luke's addition (in Lk 18:43) to what Mark has to say.
3. With this change in mind, how would you describe Luke's view of what a proper response to healing (salvation) should be?
   What other differences between Luke's version and Mark's do you think are important?

Optional   1. The story of Zaccheus occurs only in Luke. What does this story teach about
Challenges   the meaning of discipleship in this gospel?
2. Imagine you are Zaccheus. Tell your story of the evening with Jesus.
3. Make up a "new" Ten Commandments based on the teachings of Jesus found thus far in Luke.
4. What do you learn about a Christian way of living from the "meal" stories found in Luke 14–16? Would Luke think one could worship on Sunday (at Eucharist) and be a bigot on Monday? Why/why not?

SUGGESTIONS FOR THE STUDENT

After studying this lesson, you should:

1. Be more aware of the special Lukan material which has been grouped in the "Journey Section" of this gospel.

2. Be able to identify the Lukan themes of journey, prayer, right use of wealth.

3. Understand how the placement of parables in a certain context helps determine their meaning (a review of "parable").

4. Recognize Luke's use of parables as illustrative or example stories.

Memory Verse Suggestion:

Luke 19:10 —   "And Jesus said to him [Zaccheus], 'Today salvation has come to this house because this man too is a descendant of Abraham. For the Son of Man has come to seek and to save what was lost.'"

Luke 10:38-42   Jesus with Martha and Mary

I.9: Luke19:28–20:47; 22–24

Read: Luke 19:28–20:47; 22–24; Perkins pp. 98-113.

Helpful topics in MDB: Resurrection, Body, Heaven, Ascension.

Geography Task Using map on p. 28 in your *Atlas*, locate: Jericho, Bethany, Emmaus.

1. What do you learn about the identity of Jesus in this gospel from Luke's addition of the dialogue between Jesus and the thief in 23:39-43?

2. Based on your reading of Luke 24:13-35 (the "Journey to Emmaus" story), what are the different ways we can recognize the presence of the risen Lord in our lives?

3. How does the portrait of Jesus in Luke's passion story differ from the portrait of Jesus in Mark's passion story? Which portrait is more meaningful for you? Why?

4. Lukan Themes: Healing/Forgiveness/Reconciliation
   What incidents in this week's reading from Luke demonstrate this theme? After considering these incidents, what one comment would you like to make?

5. In Luke 24:4-8, what do the two men help the women realize and remember? (Note that this is also what Luke's community should realize and remember!)

Small Group Exercise Gospel Parallels Work
1. Locate Luke 19:28-38 in your *Synopsis of the Four Gospels*.
2. Note the differences in what the people say in each version.
3. What do you think Luke emphasizes in his version?

1. Locate Luke 23:44-49 in your *Synopsis of the Four Gospels*.
2. Note the last words of Jesus in each version.
3. What Lukan themes are emphasized in the additions/changes found in Luke 23:47-48?

Optional Challenges
1. Present in a written or artistic form your experience of Luke.
2. Select any scene from Luke's resurrection material and describe how you may have experienced a similar occurrence in your own life.
3. How does the dialogue between Jesus and the women of Jerusalem (23:27-31) reveal Luke's understanding of the meaning of the passion?

SUGGESTIONS FOR THE STUDENT

After studying this lesson, you should:

1. Recognize how Luke's passion and resurrection narratives have been shaped to express the major themes of his gospel, in particular his portrait of Jesus and his understanding of genuine discipleship.

2. Understand Luke's passion framework and be able to compare and contrast it with Mark's. See "An Outline of Luke's Passion," #14 in your SUPPLEMENTARY READINGS.

3. Be able to identify the structure and themes of Luke's resurrection narrative and how this narrative leads into Acts.

Memory Verse Suggestion:

Luke 23:46-47 —   "Jesus cried out in a loud voice, 'Father, into your hands I commend my spirit.' And when he had said this, he breathed his last. The centurion who witnessed what had happened glorified God and said, 'Certainly this man was innocent.'"

Other Exercises:

— Review the basic information about Luke's gospel by using "The Gospel According to Luke: Overview," #12 in your SUPPLEMENTARY READINGS.
— Do the Self-Quiz on Luke, # 15 in your SUPPLEMENTARY READINGS.
— Examine "A Chronology of the Events of Holy Week," # 13 in your SUPPLEMENTARY READINGS in order to think about how the passion accounts were put together by the evangelists.

Luke 22:47-48 Judas' betrayal of Jesus

I.10: Unit Review

The goal of this review is to make sure that the basic information about each gospel is thoroughly familiar to you. This is the kind of information which should always be remembered.

1. In preparation for the information retrieval exercise, review
    a) Overviews on the gospels of Mark (# 7) and Luke (# 12) and the Self-Quiz questions (# 15) of your SUPPLEMENTARY READINGS.
    b) Geography: Be able to locate these places and areas on a map of the Holy Land: Sea of Galilee, Dead Sea, Galilee, Samaria, Judea, Decapolis, Nazareth, Caesarea Philippi, Capernaum, Gerasa, Tyre, Sidon, Bethany, Jericho, Nain, Bethlehem, Syria, Bethsaida, Emmaus, Mount of Olives.

2. Review your memory verse from Mark's gospel and choose another from the gospel of Luke. Remember to include the chapter, verse and translation used. Pray over them as you review throughout the week, and practice writing them out for the exam.

Luke 6:44   *Luke 9:62*

AN OVERVIEW OF YEAR TWO — UNIT TWO

Jesus: A Pauline View

Objectives

1. To further familiarize ourselves with the chronology, geography, social and cultural environment of early Christianity.
2. To understand the Christian message through an investigation of the structure, themes, and theology of Acts of the Apostles and Paul's letters.
3. To increase your ability to interpret and use scripture for your personal and communal prayer.

Textbooks

P. Perkins	*Reading the New Testament* (Revised Edition)
J. McKenzie	*Dictionary of the Bible* (MDB)
Hammond's	*Atlas of the Bible Lands*

Assignments

II.1   ACTS: Chapters 1–12

II.2   ACTS: Chapters 13–28

II.3   1 and 2 THESSALONIANS; PHILIPPIANS

II.4   1 CORINTHIANS

II.5   2 CORINTHIANS

II.6   GALATIANS

II.7   ROMANS: Chapters 1–4

II.8   ROMANS: Chapters 5–16

II.9   COLOSSIANS; EPHESIANS; PHILEMON

II.10 UNIT REVIEW AND EXAM

II.1: Acts 1–12

Read: Acts 1–12; Perkins pp. 255-269.

Helpful Topics in MDB: Acts of Apostles, Grace, Pentecost, Stephen, Tongue.

Geography   Using map on p. 31 in your *Atlas*, locate: Samaria, Damascus, Antioch in Syria,
Task   Lydda, Joppa, Caesarea (not Caesarea Philippi), Phoenicia, Cyprus, Cilicia. On p.
33, locate: Cyrene, Alexandria. Using various maps, locate the places mentioned
in Acts 2:9-11.

1. How is Luke's description of the Pentecost event in 2:1-12 influenced by the
    following scenes from the Old Testament:
    a) the appearance of Yahweh on Sinai in Exodus 19:16-19
    b) the Tower of Babel incident in Genesis 11:1-11

2. a) Using the descriptions and events found in chapter 4 of Acts, identify the
        characteristics of the early Church as Luke portrays them.
    b) How do these characteristics relate to important themes which Luke has
        emphasized in his gospel?
    c) What lesson could we learn from this for our Church today?

3. What parallels do you find between the death of Jesus and the death of
    Stephen in Acts 6:8–7:60?

4. How are Peter's speeches of 3:11-26 and 10:34-43 suitable for the different
    audiences he addresses in each speech? (Remember that these speeches are
    Luke's own rendering of what Peter said rather than an eyewitness account.)

5. Lukan Themes: The Role of the Holy Spirit
    a) Identify two passages in Acts 1-12 in which the growth and expansion of
        the Church is under the direction of the Holy Spirit?
    b) Where do you perceive the influence of the Holy Spirit in our Church today?

Small Group   (This does not have to be written out but must be prepared for your small group
Exercise   discussion. Your group facilitator will report on this exercise during class.)

Paul's experience of the risen Lord is described for the first time in chapter 9 of
Acts. Based on this account:
a) On what is Paul riding?
b) What does Paul see? What does Paul tell us he saw in 1 Corinthians 9:1 and 15:8?

Optional   1. How would you reconcile the commission of the risen Lord in Acts 1:8 with
Challenges   the apparent ignorance and surprise of the disciples at the Church's turning
                      toward the Gentiles in Acts 1–12?
                  2. Compare the portrayal of Peter in Acts 1–12 with his portrayal in either
                      Mark's or Luke's gospel.
                  3. Render in a prayer or art form any one of the following:
                      Pentecost event; Saul experiencing the risen Lord; story of Stephen.

SUGGESTIONS FOR THE STUDENT

After studying this lesson, you should:

1. Understand why Luke wrote Acts, its overall structure and its essential relation to the gospel of Luke. For an outline of this book, see "The Acts of the Apostles: Overview," # 16 in your SUPPLEMENTARY READINGS.

2. Understand the role and theology of the Holy Spirit from Luke's perspective.

3. Know that the following are major themes in Acts:
   1) the growth and development of the early Church
   2) the movement to include the Gentiles
   3) the role of Peter in the early Church

Memory Verse Suggestion:

Acts 1:8 —   "You will receive power when the Holy Spirit comes down on you. Then you will be my witnesses in Jerusalem, throughout Judea and Samaria, yes, even to the ends of the earth."

Acts 3:1-10   Peter and John cure man

II.2: Acts 13–28

Read: Acts 13–28; Perkins pp. 114-147. Read also "Paul the Man and His Letters," by Sr. Macrina Scott, # 17 in your SUPPLEMENTARY READINGS.

Helpful topics in MDB: Epistle, Paul, Hellenism, Writing.

Geography Task   As you read Acts 13–28, keep your *Atlas* handy (note maps on pp. 32 and 33) and trace the journeys of Paul. Note especially the locations of: Antioch of Syria, Cyprus, Antioch in Pisidia, Galatia, Macedonia, Athens, Corinth, Crete, Malta, Rome.

1. What seems to be the pattern of Paul's missionary activity as it unfolds in chapter 13? Please give references.

2. Using the two accounts of Paul preaching to a totally Gentile audience in Acts 14:15-17 and Acts 17:22-31, please summarize how Paul describes God and what God's relationship to the Gentiles has been in the past. Also, what is the relationship between God and the Gentiles *now*, as Paul speaks of it in Acts 17:30?

3. What is said in Paul's farewell speech to the elders of Ephesus (Acts 20:17-38) that you feel would be helpful to pastors of Christian communities today?

4. Paul's defense in Acts 26 provides a summary of many of the themes in Acts. In this speech what does Paul say about:
   a) the most significant difference between Jews and Christians?
   b) the origins of Christianity in Judaism?
   c) the reasons for the Christian mission to the Gentiles?

5. What passage from Acts 13–28 gives you encouragement as you attempt to spread the Good News of Jesus Christ in your own life? Why?

Small Group Exercise   Luke gives his account of the Council in Jerusalem in Acts 15:1-21.
Paul's remembrance of this meeting can be found in Galatians 2:1-10.
   a) What differences do you find between these two accounts?
   b) Why do you think these differences exist?

Optional Challenge

1. What similarities can you find between the trial of Jesus as described in Luke's gospel and the trials of Paul as found in Acts 24–25?
2. Portray Paul in some art/prayer/literary form as you understand him from reading Acts.
3. Write a brief account of how Paul's preaching might have affected you as a first-century Gentile living in Athens.

SUGGESTIONS FOR THE STUDENT

After studying this lesson, you should:

1. See Paul as representative of the Church's turn to the Gentile nations.

2. Begin to sort out Luke's portrait of Paul from Paul's own view.

3. Understand how Luke continues the theological themes from his gospel in the Acts of the Apostles, in particular the modeling of Paul on Jesus and having Paul proclaim in his speeches the theological views of Luke.

Memory Verse Suggestion:

Acts 17:27-28 — "They [the Gentiles] were to seek God, yes to grope for him and perhaps eventually find him — though God is not far from any of us, since in him we live and move and have our being, as some of your own poets have said, for we too are God's offspring."

Other Exercises:

On the map of "The World of Paul," # 18 in your SUPPLEMENTARY READINGS, fill in for yourself the journeys that Paul makes as described in these chapters of Acts. Compare your findings with the maps of Paul's journeys found in your *Atlas*.

Study "A Chronology of Paul's Life," # 19 in your SUPPLEMENTARY READINGS, in order to situate Paul's life and letters in the historical events of the first century.

Acts 16:13-15 Paul preaches to women

II.3: 1 and 2 Thessalonians; Philippians

Read: 1 and 2 Thessalonians; Philippians; Perkins pp. 150-159. Read also "Six Letters from St. Paul" by Steve Mueller, # 21 in your SUPPLEMENTARY READINGS. An overview of each of Paul's letters is found in # 22 in your SUPPLEMENTARY READINGS.

Helpful topics in MDB: Philippi, Philippians, Thessalonians.

Geography Task Using map on p. 36 in your *Atlas*, locate: Thessalonica, Achaia, Philippi.

1. What do you learn about the early Christian community from the first chapter of 1 Thessalonians?

2. Compare and contrast 1 Thessalonians 5:1-12 with 2 Thessalonians 2:1-12 concerning the Parousia (i.e. the second and final coming) of Jesus.

3. What are some equivalents in our society to the pagan idols mentioned in 1 Thessalonians 1:9?

4. In Philippians 2:6-11, Paul uses an early Christian hymn about Christ. According to this hymn:
   a) What are the three major stages of Christ's existence?
   b) In what primary way does Christ "empty himself"?
   c) What is the name given to Christ?

   According to you:
   d) Summarize the message of this hymn in the context of this letter.

5. Philippians, with its many stirring passages, is often quoted. Which passage from this book is most meaningful for you? Why?

Small Group Exercise In the scripture reading for this week, Paul's view is that the Christian life is lived in the expectation of the Parousia. How should we interpret this view today, especially if we normally do not consider Christ's return to be imminent?

Optional Challenges
1. Imagine you are a member of either the Thessalonian or Philippian church and you have heard one of these letters read to your community. Write a return letter to Paul concerning any appropriate issue.
2. What would be Christian equivalents to the virtues admired in the pagan Greek world as found in Philippians 4:8?

SUGGESTIONS FOR THE STUDENT

After studying this lesson, you should:

1. Understand that Paul's letters are responses to immediate problems in various communities at that time. For guidelines on reading Paul, see "How To Get to the Heart of a Pauline Letter," # 20 in your SUPPLEMENTARY READINGS.

2. Notice that Paul uses many images to understand the person and especially the saving work of Jesus Christ. For a fuller chart of many of the "Images of Salvation Used by Paul," see # 23 in your SUPPLEMENTARY READINGS.

3. Be aware of the situations of the Thessalonian and Philippian communities, of the problems they were experiencing which prompted Paul's letters, and of the solutions which Paul presented in the letters.

Memory Verse Suggestion:

1 Thessalonians 1:2-3 — "We keep thanking God for all of you and we remember you in our prayers, always remembering your work of faith and labor of love and endurance in hope, before our God and Father."

2 Thessalonians 1:11 — "We pray for you always that our God may make you worthy of his call, and by his power fulfill all your desires for goodness, and complete all that you have been doing through faith."

Philippians 3:7-8 — "But those things I used to consider gain I have now reappraised as loss in the light of Christ. I have come to rate all as loss in the light of the surpassing knowledge of my Lord Jesus Christ."

You might also wish to memorize the beautiful early Christian hymn that Paul uses in Philippians 2:5-11.

Philippians 2:10-11   "Jesus is Lord"

II.4: 1 Corinthians

Read: 1 Corinthians; Perkins pp. 175-186; "House Churches and the Eucharist," by Jerome Murphy-O'Connor, # 24 in your SUPPLEMENTARY READINGS.

Helpful topics in MDB: Body, Corinth, 1 Corinthians, Divorce, Eucharist, Grace, Knowledge, Love, Resurrection, Spirit, Wisdom.

Geography Task   Using maps on p. 32 and p. 33 of your *Atlas*, locate: Corinth, Ephesus.

1. In chapters 1-4:
    a) What causes divisions in the community?
    b) How does Paul think unity can be achieved?
    c) How would his advice help the situation (as you see it) in the Church today?

2. In chapters 7-11: Choose *one* problem Paul responds to and identify:
    a) the root or cause of the problem.
    b) Paul's particular advice concerning this problem.
    c) what you see as a modern equivalent to this problem.

3. In chapters 12-14: Paul writes about spiritual gifts.
    a) What are Paul's criteria for evaluating any spiritual gift and determining which gifts take priority over others?
    b) What does the body imagery indicate about the spiritual gifts?
    c) What does 1 John 4:8 add to your understanding of 1 Corinthians 13?

4. Answer *one* of the following:
    a) 1 Corinthians is a letter full of quotable quotes and memorable passages. Which passage is most meaningful for you? Why?
    b) Write a short letter to your own local church community in the style of 1 Corinthians, addressing a situation within the community which you see as problematic.

Small Group Exercise   Paul presents his account of the Christian eucharistic words in 1 Corinthians 11:23-26. Compare and contrast his account with that of the synoptics. (Your *Synopsis of the Four Gospels* will be most helpful in doing this.)
    a) Which of the synoptic accounts is most similar to Paul's?
    b) What do you think the primary meaning of this meal is for Paul?

Optional Challenges   1. Express your "most meaningful passage" in some prayer or art form.
    2. What passages can you cite from 1 Corinthians which show Paul's use of the theme of "building"?
    3. Compare and contrast Paul's church at Corinth with the Jerusalem church as it is described in Luke's summary statements of Acts 2:42-47; 4:32-37; and 5:12-16. Which picture do you think is more realistic?

SUGGESTIONS FOR THE STUDENT

After studying this lesson, you should:

1. Understand more clearly the situation and problems of the Corinthian community for which this letter offers solutions. For a helpful formulation of this, see "What the Corinthians Said to Paul," # 25 in your SUPPLEMENTARY READINGS.

2. Be growing in your awareness of Paul's teaching method in his letters.

3. Be aware of the Pauline themes of love, wisdom, and the uniqueness of being Christian.

Memory Verse Suggestion:

1 Corinthians 1:22-25 — "Yes, Jews demand signs, and Greeks look for wisdom, but we preach Christ crucified — a stumbling block to Jews, and an absurdity to Gentiles. But to those who are called, Jews and Greeks alike, Christ is the power of God and the wisdom of God. For God's folly is wiser than human wisdom, and God's weakness stronger than human strength."

1 Corinthians 1:10   Paul speaks against factions

II.5: 2 Corinthians

Read: 2 Corinthians; Perkins pp.186-190.

Helpful topics in MDB: Apostle, 2 Corinthians, Hope.

Geography   Using maps on p. 32 and p. 36 of your *Atlas*, locate: Corinth, Troas, Macedonia.
Task

1. In chapters 3–5, Paul describes the New Covenant ministry of the gospel.
    According to chapter 4:
    a) How does one receive this ministry? (note also 3:4-6)
    b) What is the message to be preached?
    c) How does God use the "humanity" ("frailty") of the minister?

2. 2 Corinthians 5:18-21 can be seen as a summary of Paul's view of salvation
    history. According to this passage:
    a) How does Paul describe God's saving action?
        (i.e. WHAT does God do;
               what are the EFFECTS of this action;
               what MEANS does God use to do it.)
    b) What is *our* role in God's work of salvation?

3. In chapters 8–9, Paul writes about Christian generosity. In these chapters:
    a) What motives for generosity does Paul use in order to encourage the
        Corinthians in their giving?
    b) What do you learn about Paul's idea of what "church" is?

4. Based on your reading of chapters 11 and 12, how would you summarize the
    differences between "false" apostles and "true" apostles?

5. Imagine you are a newly-baptized member of the Corinthian Christian com-
    munity. Briefly describe your impressions of Paul as a pastor.

6. Choose a memory verse (including chapter, verse and translation used) from
    one of the letters of Paul that we have studied so far. Recite it for your small
    group and share with them why you chose this verse.

Small Group   Paul uses the image of "new creation" in speaking of what happens to one who is
Exercise   "in Christ" (see 2 Cor 5:17). In what ways is this notion related to the Genesis
                    accounts of creation?

Optional   1. What characteristics for Christian leadership are found in chapters 1–4?
Challenges   2. Which passage from 2 Corinthians is most meaningful for you? Why?
                    3. Reflect on 2 Corinthians 1:3-7 and 2:5-11. Express in an artistic, literary or
                        prayer form the meaning that one or both of these passages has for you.

SUGGESTIONS FOR THE STUDENT

After studying this lesson, you should:

1. Know the major themes of 2 Corinthians.

2. Understand Paul's view of himself as an apostle, his view of what an apostle is, and the importance of his role as an apostle in the community.

3. Continue to see how Paul relates his theology to practical problems.

4. Grow in your appreciation of how essential community was for the early Church.

5. For a helpful review of the unit so far, do "Paul: Self-Quiz 1," # 26 in your SUPPLEMENTARY READINGS.

Memory Verse Suggestion:

2 Corinthians 4:7-11 —   "We hold this treasure in earthen vessels, to make clear that its surpassing power comes from God and not from us. We are afflicted in every way possible, but we are not crushed, full of doubts, we never despair. We are persecuted but never abandoned; we are struck down but never destroyed. Continually we carry about in our bodies the dying of Jesus so that in our bodies the life of Jesus may also be revealed."

Underlying the metaphors and common to most of them (in ch. 2-5) is Paul's basic intuition about the essence of the spiritual life, namely, that the life-giving power or spirit that comes from the Father through the risen Christ is a power that makes all who believe in Christ one with Christ and with one another in such a way that they are literally a new humanity or a new creation.

— Peter Ellis, Seven Pauline Letters, *p. 146*

2 Corinthians 11:33   "Let down in a basket..."

II.6: Galatians

Read: Galatians; Perkins pp. 160-168.

Helpful topics in MDB: Circumcision, Freedom, Galatia, Galatians, Law.

Geography   Using maps on p. 33 and p. 36 in your *Atlas*, locate: Galatia, Arabia.
Task

1. Based on your reading of 1:11–2:10:
    a) Summarize what Paul says regarding the authority of his message and apostleship.
    b) How does Paul emphasize his "independence from" the Jerusalem church?
    c) How does Paul emphasize his concern to "work with" the Jerusalem church?

2. In chapter 3:
    a) Why does Paul appeal to the example of Abraham?
    b) What function did the Law have in the past, and why is it no longer applicable?

3. In 4:1-11:
    a) How is the ongoing relationship between God and the Christian described?
    b) What is the role of each member of the "Trinity" in this ongoing relationship?

4. In your own words, describe one modern-day example of the flesh-spirit struggle which Paul speaks of in 5:16–6:8.

5. In your own words, summarize what you feel to be THE important message of this letter.

Small Group   How would you reconcile Roman Catholic practices and observances with what
Exercise   Paul has to say in Galatians 4:8-11?

Optional   1. What passages and advice from Galatians are helpful in our efforts to preserve
Challenges   the gospel against the distortion of legalism?
                     2. What does the image of "sowing and reaping" in 6:7-8 contribute to Paul's
                         teaching on "justification by faith not works"?
                     3. Compare Paul's attitude in 3:28 with that of Rabbi Jehuda ben Elai (c. 150
                         A.D.) who wrote:
                         "Three thanksgivings must be said every day:
                         Praised be God that He has not made me a woman.
                         Praised be God that He has not made me ignorant.
                         Praised be God that He has not made me a Gentile,
                         for all Gentiles are like nothing before Him."

SUGGESTIONS FOR THE STUDENT

After studying this lesson, you should:

1. Understand the background of the Galatian community and its problems which Paul is addressing in this letter.

2. Understand Paul's movement beyond Judaism and its Law as necessary for Gentile converts.

3. See from Paul's point of view how freedom and authority operate together in a community.

Memory Verse Suggestion:

Galatians 3:26-28 — "All of you are the children of God, through faith, in Christ Jesus, since you who have been baptized in Christ have clothed yourselves with him. There does not exist among you Jew or Greek, slave or free person, male and female, for you are all one in Christ Jesus."

Galatians 2:11-14   Paul confronts Peter

II.7: Romans 1–4

Read: Romans 1–4; Perkins pp. 168-174.

Helpful topics in MDB: Free, Freedom; Law (see II. The Pauline Writings); Righteous, Righteousness; Rome; Romans (Epistle to).

Geography   Using maps on p. 33 and p. 36 in your *Atlas*, locate: Rome.
Task

1. According to 1:18-32:
   a) How can the Gentiles "know" God?
   b) How have the Gentiles responded to God and what is the result of their response?

2. According to 2:17–3:20:
   a) How can the Jews "know" God?
   b) How have the Jews responded to God and what is the result of their response?

3. Using the material found in chapters 1–4 of Romans:
   a) What does God do for humanity?
   b) How ought humanity respond to God?

4. Do you think we can understand Church law and the obligations it imposes to be equivalent to the "Law" as this term is used in this letter? Why or why not?

5. Which passage from Romans 1–4 is most meaningful for you? Why?

Small Group   In Romans 1–4 Paul shows us what damages our relations with God, others,
Exercise   and nature. Compare this reflection with that of Genesis 1–11.
   a) Where is there similarity?
   b) What one thing do you learn from this exercise?

Optional   1. Although the "works" of the liturgy and loving service to our neighbor cannot
Challenges   justify us without the kind of faith Paul describes, are they therefore to be
                     abandoned? What is their place in the living of the Christian life?
                  2. How is Abraham a model of faith for *both* Jew and Gentile?
                  3. Based on 1:18-2:16, how is it possible to reconcile Paul's teaching about the
                     wrath of God with his assertion that all who follow their consciences will be
                     saved?

SUGGESTIONS FOR THE STUDENT

After studying this lesson, you should:

1. Understand Paul's message of salvation and why he speaks of it as he does to this Roman community. (See "Images of Salvation Used by Paul," # 23 in your SUPPLEMENTARY READINGS.)

2. Understand the structure of Romans and Part 1 (chapters 1–4) in particular.

3. Understand Paul's view that salvation comes from Christ and faith, not from the Law and its observance.

4. Be able to define *justification* as God's action through Christ to bring us into the right relationship with God. Our response to this is *faith*.

Memory Verse Suggestion:

Romans 1:16-17 —   "I am not ashamed of the gospel. It is the power of God for the salvation of everyone who believes — the Jew first, then the Greek. For in the gospel is revealed the righteousness of God from faith to faith, as scripture says, 'The one who is righteous by faith shall live.'"

Romans 3:15   "...quick to shed innocent blood."

II.8: Romans 5–16

Read: Romans 5–16.

                    Helpful topics in MDB: Adam, Election, Life, Salvation, Spirit.

Geography   Review destinations of the Pauline letters on your maps.
Task

1. In 6:1–7:6, how does Paul stress that the way we live after we have been justified by faith is very important?

2. According to chapters 9–11 (Paul's concern about why Jews have not become Christians):
    a) Does God keep the divine promises made to Israel? (Explain)
    b) Is God unjust in the "election" of one person rather than another? (Explain the reasons for your answer.)
    c) What "good" results from Israel's "failure"?

3. Compare and contrast Paul's attitude toward the state as expressed in Romans 13:1-7 with Jesus' attitude as expressed in Mark 12:13-17.

4. According to chapter 15, in what ways does the example of Jesus serve as a guide for Christian conduct?

5. Imagine you are a member of the Roman Christian community and you have just heard this letter read in its entirety. If you were to go home and tell your family something you want them to remember from this letter, what would it be?

Small Group   Paul seems to make some strong statements in Romans 13:1-2 concerning the
Exercise   Christian attitude toward civil authority.
    a) How would you reconcile what he says with what the apostles say and do in Acts 4:1-22 and 5:27-42?
    b) Reflect on this answer along with your answer to question 3 above. What conclusions do you draw from your reflection?

Optional   1. In Romans 6:1-11, how does the baptism ritual demonstrate our belief that
Challenges   our own inevitable death is not the "end"?
                    2. How does Paul's attitude in Romans 8:31-39 help us today as we face the possibility of the nuclear destruction of our planet?
                    3. In what sense are we Christians today to consider ourselves "free from the law" as Paul claims in Romans 7:6?

SUGGESTIONS FOR THE STUDENT

After studying this lesson, you should:

1. Be more knowledgeable about Paul's view of the spiritual life, and recognize the contrasting images in which Paul presents it.

2. Understand Paul's idea of salvation's effects on us now.

3. Understand Paul's view of the Jews and their continuing place/role in God's plan.

4. Continue to see the importance of applying the Christian message to practical life situations, as well as seeing that this is exactly what Paul attempts to do by giving advice and encouragement in his letters.

5. Be able to define *sanctification* as God's action through the Holy Spirit to transform us and our world.

Memory Verse Suggestion:

Romans 8:28 — "We know that all things work for good for those who love God, who are called according to his purpose."

Romans 8:35, 38-39 — "What will separate us from the love of Christ? ... For I am certain that neither death nor life, neither angels nor principalities, neither the present nor the future, nor powers, nor height nor depth nor any other creature, will be able to separate us from the love of God in Christ Jesus, our Lord."

Romans 11:33-36 — "Oh, the depth of the riches and wisdom and knowledge of God. How inscrutable are his judgments and how unsearchable are his ways! For who has known the mind of the Lord? Or who has been his counselor? Or who has given him anything that he may be repaid? For from him and through him and for him are all things. To him be glory forever. Amen."

Romans 8:21   "The whole creation ... freed."

II.9: Colossians, Ephesians, Philemon

Read:

Colossians; Ephesians; Philemon; Perkins pp. 191-202 and 147-150 (middle); and "Six More Letters from St. Paul," by Steve Mueller, # 27 in your SUPPLEMENTARY READINGS.

Helpful topics in MDB: Church, Colossae (Colossians), Ephesus (Ephesians), Mystery, Philemon.

Geography Task

Using maps on p. 33 and p. 36 in your *Atlas*, locate: Colossae, Ephesus, Laodicea.

1. What is Christ's "place" in the Christian view of reality according to the christological hymn of Colossians 1:15-20?

2. In your own words, summarize God's plan for salvation as you understand it from Ephesians 1-3.

3. Ephesians 5:22–6:9 and Colossians 3:18–4:1, known as "household codes," give advice on practical situations found within various types of relationships. Based upon your reading of these passages:
    a) What motivation does Paul offer for the type of behavior he expects of Christians?
    b) Do you find the principle of "equality in God's sight" present in these passages? Briefly explain your answer.

4. What does Paul's letter to Philemon have to say about a Christian attitude toward slavery?

5. What do you feel are the most important insights you have gained in your study of the Pauline letters?

Small Group Exercise

Ephesians 5:21-33 presents a Christian interpretation of marriage.
a) Compare and contrast this interpretation with the treatment of marriage found in 1 Corinthians 7.
b) In relation to the marriage customs of Paul's time (read MDB: Marriage), to whom is the "harder" advice given — to wives or to husbands? Why?

Optional Challenges

1. Present your personal view of Paul (both as a person and as an apostle) in some written or artistic form.
2. Compare and contrast the image of "church" as found in 1 Corinthians 12; Romans 12; and Ephesians 4.
3. Compare and contrast the use of the term "mystery" in Colossians and Ephesians.
4. During the 19th-century debate over slavery in the United States, some used the letter of Philemon to justify the institution of slavery. Do you agree with this use of this letter or not? Give reasons for your position.

SUGGESTIONS FOR THE STUDENT

After studying this lesson, you should:

1. Understand why Paul's own authorship of Colossians and Ephesians is questioned and what are possible solutions to this problem.

2. Understand the occasion for these letters and what major themes are found in them.

3. Be growing in your ability to summarize salvation history and God's relation to us.

Memory Verse Suggestion:

Colossians 3:1-4 — "Since you have been raised with Christ, seek what is above, where Christ is seated at God's right hand. Think of what is above, not of what is of earth. For you have died! Your life is hidden now with Christ in God. When Christ your life appears, then you too shall appear with him in glory."

Ephesians 3:16-19 — "May God grant you in accord with the riches of his glory to be strengthened with power through his spirit in your inner self. May Christ dwell in your hearts through faith, that you, rooted and grounded in love, may have strength to comprehend with all the holy ones what is the breadth and length and height and depth, and to know the love of Christ that surpasses knowledge, so that you may be filled with the fullness of God."

Philemon 6-7 — "My prayer is that your sharing of the faith with others may enable you to know all the good which is ours in Christ. I find great joy and comfort in your love, because through you the hearts of God's people have been refreshed."

Ephesians 6:1 "Children, be obedient to your parents."

II.10: Unit Review

The goal of this review is to make sure that the basic information about each book is thoroughly familiar to you. This is the kind of information which should always be remembered.

1. In preparation for the information retrieval exercise, review
    a) Overviews of Acts (# 16) and of the letters of Paul (# 22) and "Images of Salvation Used by Paul" (# 23) in your SUPPLEMENTARY READINGS.
    b) "Paul: Self-Quiz 1" (# 26), "Paul: Self-Quiz 2" (# 28) and "Paul: Self-Quiz 3" (# 29) in your SUPPLEMENTARY READINGS.

2. Geography: Be able to locate these places and areas on the map of "The World of Paul" (# 18 in your SUPPLEMENTARY READINGS): Damascus in Syria, Antioch in Syria, Cyprus, Cilicia, Crete, Rome, Galatia, Macedonia, Corinth, Athens, Thessalonica, Ephesus, Philippi, Colossae, Tarsus.

3. Review your memory verse from the earlier letters of Paul and choose another from the letter to the Romans. Remember to include the chapter, verse and translation used. Pray over them as you review throughout the week, and practice writing them for the exam.

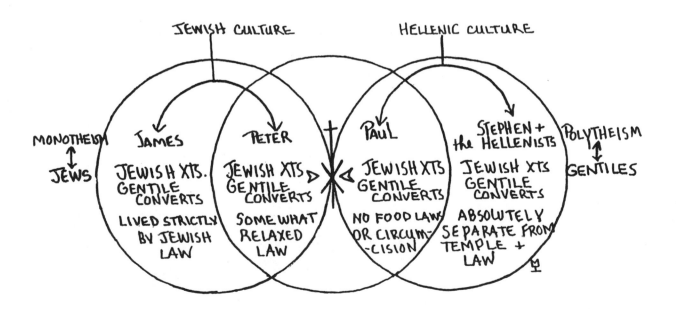

AN OVERVIEW OF YEAR TWO — UNIT THREE

Jesus: Two Johannine Views

Objectives

1. To further familiarize ourselves with the chronology, geography, social and cultural environment of early Christianity as reflected in Johannine writings.
2. To understand the Christian message through an investigation of the structure, themes and theology of the Johannine authors of John and Revelation.
3. To understand the writings of apocalyptic Christianity and to apply to them the methods of biblical criticism in order to interpret the meaning of these writings in a more adequate way.

Textbooks

P. Perkins	*Reading the New Testament* (Revised Edition)
N. Flanagan	*The Gospel According to John and the Johannine Epistles* (Collegeville Bible Commentary)
J. McKenzie	*Dictionary of the Bible* (MDB)
W. Kelber	*Mark's Story of Jesus*
S. Kealy	*The Apocalypse of John*
Hammond's	*Atlas of the Bible Lands*

Assignments

III.1 JOHN'S BOOK OF SIGNS 1: Jesus and the Response of Faith

III.2 JOHN'S BOOK OF SIGNS 2: Jesus and the Jewish Feasts

III.3 JOHN'S BOOK OF GLORY 1: The Farewell Discourse

III.4 JOHN'S BOOK OF GLORY 2: Passion, Death, Resurrection

III.5 APOCALYPTIC CHRISTIANITY: Mark 13; Luke 21; Matthew 24–25

III.6 REVELATION 1–3

III.7 REVELATION 4–11

III.8 REVELATION 12:1–19:10

III.9 REVELATION 19:11–22:21

III.10 UNIT REVIEW AND EXAM

III.I: John's Book of Signs 1 — Jesus and the Response of Faith

Read:

John 1–4; Perkins pp. 242-254; Flanagan, introductory material and commentary on chapters 1–4.

Helpful topics in MDB: Baptism, Blood, Bread, Darkness, Eucharist, Faith, Flesh, Hour, John (Gospel), Judgment, Lamb, Life, Light, Love, Manna, Sign, Sin, Spirit, Water, Witness, Word.

Geography Task

Using map on p. 36 in your *Atlas*, locate: Ephesus. On p. 26, locate: Cana, Bethany, Bethsaida, Samaria, Sychar, Judea, Galilee, Jerusalem.

1. What does the Prologue of John 1:1-18 tell you about the identity of the Word (who the Word is) and the work of the Word (what the Word does)?

2. What do you learn about the identity of Jesus from:
   a) the marriage feast at Cana incident? (John 2:1-12)
   b) the cleansing of the temple incident? (John 2:13-22)

3. Johannine Themes: A major theme is the Response of Faith to Jesus.
   a) Please choose *one* of the following characters: Jesus' mother; Nicodemus; Samaritan woman at well; the royal official.
   b) Briefly discuss their faith-response to Jesus. (e.g. How would you describe their faith attitude? Does it change during the story [how]? Does this person demonstrate adequate or inadequate faith? Etc.)

4. Which passage from John 1–4 best reflects your understanding of who Jesus is? Why did you choose this passage?

Small Group Exercise

John and the Synoptics
(This does not have to be written out but must be prepared for your small group discussion. Your group facilitator will report on this exercise during class.)

Contrast the call of the first disciples in John 1:35-51 with the call story found in Mark 1:16-20. (See *Synopsis*, pp. 21f)

Optional Challenges

1. Portray the Prologue in some prayer or art form.
2. How does the evangelist use "creation" themes in chapters 1–2?
3. In what ways does the evangelist stress the subordination of John the Baptist to Jesus?

SUGGESTIONS FOR THE STUDENT

After studying this lesson, you should:

1. Know the approximate date of writing for this gospel, the probable location and the situation of the Johannine community. For further information see "The History of the Johannine Community," # 30 in your SUPPLEMENTARY READINGS.

2. Understand the tension of Christianity/Judaism after the destruction of the temple and see John's gospel as a response to this tension.

3. Begin to appreciate the contribution of John as author of this gospel, and to recognize the many distinctive ways in which this gospel is unlike the synoptic gospels. For a helpful summary of the "Characteristic Style and Vocabulary: Gospel According to John," see # 31 in your SUPPLEMENTARY READINGS.

Memory Verse Suggestion:

John 3:5-8 —   "Jesus answered: 'Amen, Amen I say to you, no one can enter the kingdom of God without being born of water and Spirit. What is born of flesh is flesh and what is born of spirit is spirit. Do not be amazed that I told you that you must be born from above.'"

> *The "Seven Signs" in John:*
>
> *1)   Changing of water into wine at Cana (2:1-11)*
> *2)   Curing the official's son at Cana (4:46-54)*
> *3)   Curing the paralytic at Bethesda (5:1-15)*
> *4)   Miraculous feeding in Galilee (6:1-15)*
> *5)   Walking on water (6:16-21)*
> *6)   Curing the man born blind (9:1-41)*
> *7)   Raising Lazarus from the dead (11:1-53)*

John 1:36   "Look! There is the lamb of God!"

III.2: John's Book of Signs 2 — Jesus and the Jewish Feasts

Read: John 5–12; Flanagan commentary on chapters 5–12.

Geography   Using map on p. 28 in your *Atlas*, locate: Capernaum. On p. 29, locate: Pool
Task   of Bethesda, Solomon's Portico.

1. In chapter 5, how does the evangelist show that Jesus is both equal to God and yet subordinate to God?

2. Choose *one* of the Jewish feasts mentioned in chapters 6–10 and:
   a) Give Old Testament reference(s) which provide background for the feast and its celebration in the time of Jesus; then summarize the meaning of the feast in your own words. (For information see MDB and "Jewish Calendar and Special Feast Days," # 32 in your SUPPLEMENTARY READINGS.)
   b) Show how in John's gospel Jesus is presented as the fulfillment of the meaning and symbolism of the Jewish feast you selected.

3. Why do the "I AM" statements of Jesus in chapter 8 bother "the Jews" so much?

4. Johannine Themes: A major theme in these chapters is Life.
   Briefly describe what Life means as you understand it from these chapters. Give references to chapter and verse for the passages you use as the basis for your answer.

Small Group   John and the Synoptics
Exercise   Contrast the Anointing at Bethany scene in John 12:1-8 with similar incidents
                   found in Mark 14:3-9 and Luke 7:36-50. (See *Synopsis*, p. 277.)
                   a) What differences do you find in the three stories?
                   b) What message does each evangelist stress in his version?

Optional   1. Use either prose, poetry, prayer, or some art form to portray Jesus as you
Challenges   understand him from your study of the "Book of Signs."
                   2. The "sign" in 5:1-15 seems to be a failure because no faith in Jesus results.
                      What does this failure reveal about Jesus and his mission?
                   3. How do the passages of 5:23-30 and 12:31, 44-50 show the distinctive Johannine theology of God's judgment of the world?

SUGGESTIONS FOR THE STUDENT

After studying this lesson, you should:

1. Recognize how John shows Jesus replacing Jewish feasts with himself.

2. See how Jesus is portrayed in this gospel as being equal to God, but that he is *not* the Father.

Memory Verse Suggestion:

John 12:23-26 — "Jesus answered them: 'The hour has come for the Son of Man to be glorified. Amen, amen, I say to you, unless a grain of wheat falls to the ground and dies, it remains just a grain of wheat. But if it dies, it produces much fruit. Whoever loves their life loses it, and whoever hates their life in this world will preserve it for eternal life. Whoever serves me must follow me, and where I am, there also will my servant be. The Father will honor whoever serves me.'"

"I AM" sayings in John:

6:20	*"He called out, 'I AM; do not be afraid.'"*
8:23	*"I AM from above. Your home is in this world; I AM not..."*
8:24	*"If you do not believe that I AM, you will die in your sins."*
8:28	*"When you have lifted up the Son of Man you will know I AM."*
8:58	*"Before Abraham came to be, I AM."*
13:19	*"I tell you this now...so that...you may believe I AM."*
18:5	*"Jesus said, 'I AM.'"*

ALSO NOTE: 4:26; 6:35, 51; 8:12; 9:5; 10:7, 9, 11, 14; 11:25; 14:6; 15:1, 5.

John 11:20   Martha goes to meet Jesus

III.3: John's Book of Glory 1 — The Farewell Discourse

Read: John 13–17; Flanagan commentary on chapters 13–17.

Helpful topics in MDB: Eucharist, Lord, Paraclete, Spirit, Teacher, Truth, Word, World.

1. Although John does not portray the Last Supper as a Passover meal, what do you learn from John's account of Jesus' Last Supper in chapter 13 which gives deeper meaning to our commemoration of the Last Supper (our "Eucharist" or Mass)?

2. According to the views of the evangelist in chapters 15 and 17, what does it mean to be a Christian community, i.e. what is the community's relationship with Jesus and what is the community's mission?

3. Johannine Themes: The fourth evangelist paints a distinctive portrait of the Paraclete who is to come after Jesus returns to the Father. Summarize the Johannine view of the identity and mission of this Paraclete, using the following passages as reference: John 14:16-18, 25-26; 15:26-27; and 16:1-16.

4. Please choose *one* of the following options and give your response:
   a) Compare Jesus' last discourse in these chapters to another "farewell discourse" that you have already studied, e.g. that of Jacob (Gen 47:29–49:33), Moses (the book of Deuteronomy), Joshua (Jos 22–24), or Paul (Acts 20:17-38).
   b) Write your own "Farewell Discourse" to a specific individual or group. Emphasize what you want them to remember about you and what you want them to carry on in their lives from your life experience.

5. Which passage from this week's reading in John is most meaningful for you? Why?

Optional Challenges

1. How does John 14:1-11 confirm the evangelist's view of Jesus as the one who reveals God?
2. How could Christians do "greater things" than Jesus, as promised in John 14:12?

SUGGESTIONS FOR THE STUDENT

After studying this lesson, you should:

1. Know and appreciate the differences between the Last Supper scene in John and the synoptics, noting especially in John: the Farewell Discourse and foot washing scene and what this gospel teaches about Eucharist even without the institution scene found in the synoptics.

2. Know the Johannine understanding of the identity and mission of the Para-clete (Holy Spirit).

3. Understand the Johannine ideal of what a Christian community is and what it should be doing in the world.

4. Appreciate how the evangelist John understood the relationships of his community to other groups; see "Religious Groups Outside John's Community," # 33 in your SUPPLEMENTARY READINGS.

Memory Verse Suggestion:

John 15:5-7 —   "I am the vine, you are the branches. Whoever remains in me and I in him will bear much fruit, because without me you can do nothing. Anyone who does not remain in me will be thrown out like a branch and wither; people will gather them and throw them into a fire and they will be burned. If you remain in me and my words remain in you, ask for whatever you want and it will be done for you."

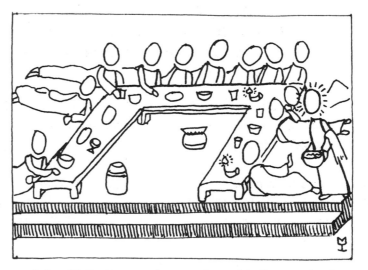

John 13:8   Peter refuses to have his feet washed

III.4: John's Book of Glory 2 — Passion, Death, Resurrection

Read: John 18–21; Flanagan commentary on chapters 18–21.

Geography   Using map on p. 29 in your *Atlas*, locate: Kidron Valley and Golgotha.
Task

1. What do you learn about the identity of Jesus from his arrest in 18:1-11?

2. In John 20:24-29:
   a) How does Thomas represent an attitude found in John's community?
   b) What relevance does this have for us today?

3. Johannine Themes: The Beloved Disciple is a very important character in this gospel and often appears with Peter. Compare and contrast the faith of the Beloved Disciple with that of Peter in the following passages: 13:21-26; 18:15-27; 19:25-30; 20:1-10; 21:1-25.

4. Portray in any prayer, art, or literary form the most important insight you have gained from this gospel. (Please pause and consider this question seriously before you answer.)

5. Select and memorize a memory verse from John's gospel. Recite it for your group and explain why you chose it.

Small Group   John and the Synoptics
Exercise   Contrast the "giving of the Spirit" as seen in John 20:21-23 with Luke's version in Acts 2:1-4. What aspect(s) of the Church's mission is emphasized in each account?

Optional   1. What does chapter 21 tell you about the Johannine community's understand-
Challenges   ing of Eucharist?
                   2. What pros and cons would there be in having John as our *only* gospel version?
                   3. John 20:31 states the purpose for writing this gospel. Give one example of how you see this purpose being carried out in chapters 1–12. Then, do the same for chapters 13–21.

Our Good Friday meditation on the "Seven Last Words of Jesus" is a compilation of the words from all of the various gospel accounts. It is also interesting to reflect how each evangelist's portrait of Jesus' death is a reinforcement of that particular evangelist's theology.

MARK:

"Eloi, Eloi, lema sabachthani?"

"My God, my God, why have you forsaken me?"

(gives a loud cry before dying)

MATTHEW:

"Eli, Eli, lema sabachthani?"

"My God, my God, why have you forsaken me?"

LUKE:

"Father, forgive them, for they know not what they do."

"Truly, I say to you, today you will be with me in paradise."

"Father, into your hands I commend my spirit."

JOHN:

"Woman, behold your son. Behold your mother."

"I thirst."

"It is finished."

SUGGESTIONS FOR THE STUDENT

After studying this lesson, you should:

1. Recognize how John's passion narrative reinforces the special theology of his gospel. For an outline of John's Passion see # 34 in your SUPPLEMENTARY READINGS.

2. Be aware of the different Holy Week chronologies in John and the synoptics. See the chart on the "Chronology of Holy Week," # 13 in your SUPPLEMENTARY READINGS.

3. Understand John's resurrection theology of Jesus and the Holy Spirit.

4. Have an appreciation of the Beloved Disciple as an important character within John's narrative (whether or not he is a real person, a symbolic figure, or a real individual idealized).

Memory Verse Suggestion:

John 20:30-31 — "Now Jesus did many other signs in the presence of the disciples that are not written in this book. But these are written that you may believe that Jesus is the Messiah, the Son of God, and that through this belief you may have life in his name."

Other Exercises:

— Review the gospel of John by studying "The Gospel According to John: Overview," # 35 in your SUPPLEMENTARY READINGS.

— Answer the questions on the the gospel of John in the Self-Quiz, # 39 in your SUPPLEMENTARY READINGS.

John 20:19-21 Jesus appears to the disciples

III.5: Apocalyptic Christianity

Read:

Mark 13; Luke 21; Matthew 24-25; Kelber pp. 66-70; Perkins pp.150-54; Kealy pp. 1-36; "Apocalyptic Literature: Overview," # 36 in your SUPPLEMENTARY READINGS.

Helpful topics in MDB: Parousia, Apocalyptic Literature, Paradise, Revelation, Gehenna, Son of Man, Day of the Lord.

1. For each of the three synoptic gospels answer the following questions: [You might find it most helpful to turn your answer paper sideways and divide it into three columns, one for each evangelist, so you can more easily see the comparisons.]
    a) To whom is Jesus speaking?
    b) Where does Jesus give his speech?
    c) What questions are asked of Jesus?
    d) What signs are to precede the fall of Jerusalem?
    e) When will the end of the world and the Parousia be?
    f) What signs are to precede this?

2. How does each evangelist indicate how we ought to use the time we have until the end comes?

3. How does each evangelist provide some hope for his community in these passages?

4. What one message seems to stand out for you from each evangelist?

5. Many first-century Jews felt as if the end of the temple would be the end of their world. What would feel like the end of the world for you?

Optional Challenges

1. Why do you think Luke might want to omit Mark 13:32? What might this omission reveal about Luke's idea of Jesus and the needs of his community?
2. How do Matthew's additional parables in chapter 25 show his understanding of the norm or standard for human conduct?
3. How does Luke's conclusion to the discourse of Jesus relate to some of his concerns throughout the rest of his gospel?
4. What might be the reason for each author's concern for the destruction of Jerusalem?

SUGGESTIONS FOR THE STUDENT

After studying this lesson, you should:

1. Understand what apocalyptic literature is, its characteristics, its relation to Judaism and the Old Testament, and what types of situation give rise to it.

2. Be aware that some Christians in the first-century communities connected the destruction of the Jerusalem temple in 70 A.D. by the Romans with the end of the world. Each of the synoptic evangelists tries very hard to separate these two events in his apocalyptic discourses.

Memory Verse Suggestion:

Mark 13:32-33 — "But of that day or hour, no one knows, neither the angels in heaven, nor the Son, but only the Father. Be watchful! Be alert! You do not know when the time will come."

[Some other memory verses which reflect the apocalyptic mentality are Romans 8:35-39 from Lesson II.8 above and John 16:33, "I have told you this so that you might have peace in me. In the world you will have trouble, but take courage, I have conquered the world."]

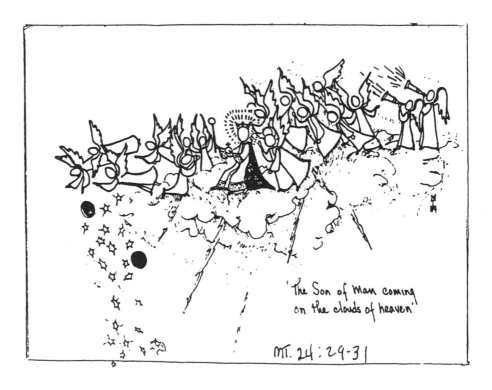

'The Son of Man coming on the clouds of heaven'

MT. 24:29-31

III.6: Revelation 1–3

Read:

Revelation 1–3; Perkins pp. 313-328; Kealy pp. 62-109; "Understanding the Book of Revelation," by Sr. Macrina Scott, # 37 in your SUPPLEMENTARY READINGS.

Helpful topics in MDB: Antichrist, Apocalypse, Babylon, Book of Life, Millennium, Number, Rome, Seal.

Geography Task

Using map on p. 37 in your *Atlas*, locate: Patmos, Ephesus, Smyrna, Pergamum, Sardis, Thyatira, Philadelphia, Laodicea.

1. In the introduction to his book (Rev 1:1-8), what does the author reveal about:
   a) the kind of book he is writing?
   b) the source of his book?
   c) the purpose of his book?

2. Themes of Revelation: The Identity of God and of Christ
   Based on your reading of chapters 1–3, describe the portrait of God *and* the portrait of Christ given to us by the author. (*Hint:* Make good use of the titles given to each as well as the characteristics describing each.)

3. Choose *one* of the "Seven Letters to the Christian Churches" found in chapters 2–3, and then answer the following questions based on the letter you have chosen:
   a) How is Christ described in this letter?
   b) For what is the church praised?
   c) For what is the church reproached?
   d) What reward is promised to the church?

4. Which of the seven churches addressed in Revelation 2–3 reminds you most of your own parish community? Why?

5. What is the most important thing you have learned about apocalyptic literature and/or the Book of Revelation?

Small Group Exercise

The Apocalypse and You
Explain how the author's purpose for writing this book is demonstrated in the seven letters of chapters 2–3.

Optional Challenges

1. Write a letter to your parish church using the same format as the seven letters found in chapters 2–3.
2. Express through any prayer or art form the portrait of God or Christ as you find it in chapters 1–3.

SUGGESTIONS FOR THE STUDENT

After studying this lesson, you should:

1. Know the probable date, place, situation of the Book of Revelation. Be aware of the clues about the identity of the author from the text.

2. Be aware of the overall structure of the Book of Revelation and of chapters 1–3 in particular.

3. Understand that the aim of the book is to generate hope because of who God is and who we are. Remember that the type of book that the author is trying to write controls the way that we have to try to interpret it. This book is a prophetic message in an apocalyptic style.

4. See within Revelation the circular letter to the seven churches as preface to the message of hope in persecution.

Memory Verse Suggestion:

Revelation 3:15-17 —   [To the church at Laodicea] "I know your works; I know that you are neither cold nor hot. I wish you were either cold or hot. So, because you are lukewarm, neither hot nor cold, I will spit you out of my mouth. For you say, 'I am rich and affluent and have no need of anything,' and yet you do not realize that you are wretched, pitiable, poor, blind, and naked."

Revelation 2:7   To feed from the tree of life

III.7: Revelation 4–11

Read: Revelation 4–11; Kealy pp. 109-164.

1. Why is the Lamb alone able to receive and unroll the sealed scroll in chapter 5?

2. Themes of Revelation: God's Power and Judgment over Creation
   Please summarize what you learn about the apocalyptic view of God's power and judgment from your reading of chapters 6 and 8 (the imagery of the first six seals and the first four trumpet blasts).

3. Which events from the book of Exodus does the author of Revelation draw upon in the following passages? (Please give citations from Exodus):
   a) Revelation 4:5-6 and 11:19
   b) Revelation 5:10
   c) Revelation 7:3
   d) Revelation 8:7-11 and 9:2-6

4. What does the story of the "little scroll" in Revelation 10 tell you about the author's experience of God and the mission God gives him?

Small Group Exercise   The Apocalypse and You
As you try to live a Christian lifestyle today, how do you reconcile the martyr's cry for vengeance in Revelation 6:10 with the advice Jesus gives in Luke 6:27?

Optional Challenges

1. Write a history of world events (e.g. World War II, the American involvement in Vietnam or in the Middle East, the succession of American presidents) using symbolism rather than proper names. Let your small group try to figure out the meaning as you read it to them.
2. In the story of chapter 11, the author portrays his understanding of what is happening in his communities at that time. How would you apply the meaning of this chapter to the life of Christian communities today?
3. What historical memories from the time of the conquest of Jerusalem by Antiochus Epiphanes (175-163 B.C.) contribute to the symbolism used by the author in chapter 11? (See MDB: Antiochus 1. for details.)
4. Express what you consider to be the main message of these chapters in some art form, prayer form or literary form.

SUGGESTIONS FOR THE STUDENT

After studying this lesson, you should:

1. Understand the apocalyptic view of the relationship between God and our world, especially in terms of God's saving activity and how the author relates the experience of his time to that of the Exodus and other scenes of salvation history.

2. Recognize the importance of paying close attention first to what the text says and what it might have meant to the original audience.

3. See that Old Testament background is absolutely essential for understanding the author's point.

4. Be more familiar with the author's use of images and symbols to convey his meaning to the audience.

Memory Verse Suggestion:

Revelation 5:11-12 — "I looked again and heard the voices of many angels who surrounded the throne and the living creatures and the elders. They were countless in number. They cried out in a loud voice: 'Worthy is the Lamb that was slain, to receive power and riches, wisdom and strength, honor and glory and blessing.'"

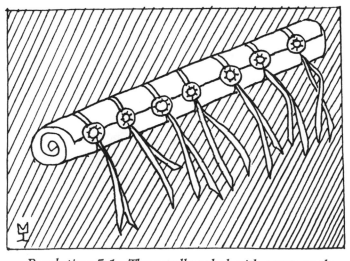

Revelation 5:1 The scroll sealed with seven seals

III.8: Revelation 12:1–19:10

Read: Revelation 12:1–19:10; Kealy pp. 165-213.

1. Based on your reading of Revelation 12:1-8:
   a) What does the biblical text *say* about the woman?
      (State your answer in your own words and be sure to use references to support what you say.)
   b) Who do you think the *woman represents*? Why? (Make sure to indicate the connections or links to the text which you are using.)

2. What enemies to the Christian community are symbolically represented in Revelation 12:1-13:18?

3. Themes of Revelation: God's Victory over Evil and God's Reward for the Just and Punishment for the Unjust
   Give examples of this theme from chapters 15 and 16. Describe the examples in your own words and give citations from the text.

4. What connections with the Exodus do you find in chapter 15?

5. Based on your reading of chapters 17 and 18 and your knowledge of Jewish history (see MDB, Exile), why do you think it is appropriate for the author to symbolize Rome as "Babylon"?

Small Group Exercise

The Apocalypse and You
How would you apply today what Revelation 12:1–19:10 says about the Christian attitude toward the state? Compare this attitude with that expressed by Paul in Romans 13.

Optional Challenges:

1. Write a brief "apocalyptic" account of the fall of a dominant power (e.g. Hitler's Germany, Soviet Russia or legal racial prejudice in the United States) from the viewpoint of the victims of that power. Remember to encode your message in symbolic images.
2. Why does the author of Revelation seem more preoccupied with *justice* than with *Christian love*?
3. What do you consider the best interpretation of the "virginity" mentioned in Revelation 14:4?

SUGGESTIONS FOR THE STUDENT

After studying this lesson, you should:

1. Be able to understand and work with symbols and their interpretation.

2. See that God and God's relation to us is an important key to the interpretation of the Book of Revelation.

3. Recognize that Revelation presents God as solution to tensions of persecution.

Memory Verse Suggestion:

Revelation 15:3-4 —   "And they sang the song of Moses, the servant of God, and the song of the Lamb:
'Great and wonderful are your works,
Lord God almighty.
Just and true are your ways,
O king of the nations.
Who will not fear you, Lord,
or glorify your name?
For you alone are holy.
All the nations will come
and worship before you,
For your righteous acts
have been revealed.'"

Revelation 12:1
A woman clothed with the sun

III.9: Revelation 19:11–22:21

Read: Revelation 19:11–22:21; Kealy pp. 213-233.

1. Based on your reading of Revelation 19:11-16:
    a) Who is Jesus?
    b) What are the works Jesus does?

2. Compare and contrast the last judgment scene of Revelation 20:11-15 with that of Matthew 25:31-46. Then, state briefly what you understand to be the main message of each scene.

3. The Bible begins and ends with "visions" of "paradise." What passages in Revelation 22 are reminiscent of the Genesis account of the Garden of Eden?

4. Themes of Revelation: Christian Hope
    Please choose *one* of the following and give your response:
    a) Based on your study of Revelation, what reasons would you give for saying that this book is meant to strengthen Christian hope?
    b) Compose your own brief apocalyptic work giving encouragement and hope to Christians attempting to live out their faith in the modern world.

Small Group Exercise

The Apocalypse and You
Now that you have studied Revelation, please share your impressions of this book. Are your feelings about this book any different now than what they were prior to this study?

Optional Challenges

1. Which passage from Revelation is most meaningful for you? Why?

2. What is the significance of the claim spoken in 22:6-20 by the angel, Jesus, and the author?

3. What do you learn about the meaning of discipleship from the seven beatitudes found in the Book of Revelation? (See 1:3, 14:13, 16:15, 19:9, 20:6, 22:7, and 22:14.)

4. John wants his last chapter to bring the reader's mind back to the first, giving a sense of completion. What common themes and phrases do you find in the first and last chapters?

SUGGESTIONS FOR THE STUDENT

After studying this lesson, you should:

1. Understand that the Book of Revelation needs to be balanced by the teaching in the rest of the Old and New Testament.

2. Be able to understand and explain the basic message and approach of the Book of Revelation together with its specific contribution to Christian life.

Memory Verse Suggestion:

Revelation 21:1-4 —   "Then I saw a new heaven and a new earth. The former heaven and the former earth had passed away, and the sea was no more. I also saw the holy city, a new Jerusalem, coming down out of heaven from God, prepared as a bride adorned for her husband. I heard a loud voice from the throne saying, 'Behold, God's dwelling is with the human race. God will dwell with them and they will be God's people and God himself will always be with them. God will wipe away every tear from their eyes, and there shall be no more death or mourning, wailing or pain, for the old order has passed away.'"

Other Exercises:

— Review the Book of Revelation by studying "The Book of Revelation: Overview," # 38 in your SUPPLEMENTARY READINGS.
— Answer the questions on the Book of Revelation in the Self-Quiz, # 39 in your SUPPLEMENTARY READINGS.

Revelation 19:17
An angel standing in the sun

III.10: Unit Review

1. In preparation for the information retrieval exercise, review
    a) The basic information concerning John's Gospel and the Book of Revelation. The overviews (# 35 and 38) in your SUPPLEMENTARY READINGS will be helpful for your review. The Self-Quiz on the Gospel of John and the Book of Revelation (# 39) will help focus the material.
    b) Geography: Be able to locate the following places and areas. See the "Map Quizzes," # 40 in your SUPPLEMENTARY READINGS:
       Cana, Judea, Bethany, Samaria, Bethsaida, Galilee, Sychar, Dead Sea, Capernaum, Sea of Tiberias (= John's name for Sea of Galilee), Patmos, Ephesus, Smyrna, Pergamum, Thyatira, Sardis, Philadelphia, Laodicea, and Rome

2. Review your memory verse from the gospel of John. Choose another memory verse from the Book of Revelation. (Remember to include the chapter, verse and translation used.) Pray over them and practice writing them out for the exam.

3. **Group Appreciation Exercise:**

    The aim of this exercise is to express your appreciation for the members of your small group.
    1) Take the name of one person from your small group. Make sure that each person in the group has someone to write about her or him.
    2) Write out a brief testimonial about the gift that person's presence has been to your group during this year. Perhaps the guidelines for writing this could be an adaptation of Ephesians 4:25-32:
       > "Therefore, putting away falsehood, speak the truth, each one to his or her neighbor, for we are members of one another.... No foul language should come out of your mouths, but only such as is good to hear.... And be kind to one another, compassionate, forgiving one another as God has forgiven you in Christ."
    3) Bring your testimonial and share it with the group next week. After sharing it with the group, present it to the person you wrote about.

SUPPLEMENTARY READINGS

In this section you will find the readings suggested for use with the assignment questions. The index below identifies the reading and the assignment for which it is used.

1. INSTRUCTION OF THE PONTIFICAL BIBLICAL COMMISSION ON THE HISTORICAL TRUTH OF THE GOSPELS (1964)

This Instruction was the basis for the more abbreviated formulation adopted by the Bishops at Vatican Council II in its Dogmatic Constitution on Divine Revelation (Dei Verbum), # 19. *It is very important to recognize the guidelines provided here for discovering the proper meaning of the scripture texts. Bold print has been added to highlight sections which are very important for your study and reflection.*

I. Holy Mother the Church "the pillar and bulwark of truth,"[1] has always used Sacred Scripture in her task of imparting heavenly salvation to human beings. She has always defended it too, from every sort of false interpretation. **Since there will never be an end to (biblical) problems, the Catholic exegete should never lose heart in explaining the divine word and in solving the difficulties proposed to him. Rather, let him strive earnestly to open up still more the real meaning of the Scriptures. Let him rely firmly not only on his own resources, but above all on the help of God and the light of the Church.**

II. It is a source of great joy that there are found today, to meet the needs of our times, faithful children of the Church in great numbers who are experts in biblical matters. They are following the exhortations of the Supreme Pontiffs and are dedicating themselves wholeheartedly and untiringly to this serious and arduous task. "Let all the other children of the Church bear in mind that the efforts of these resolute laborers in the vineyard of the Lord are to be judged not only with equity and justice, but also with the greatest charity,"[2] since even illustrious interpreters, such as Jerome himself, tried at times to explain the more difficult questions with no great success.[3] Care should be had "that the keen strife of debate should never exceed the bounds of mutual charity. Nor should the impression be given in an argument that truths of revelation and divine traditions are being called in question. For unless agreement among minds be safeguarded and principles be carefully respected, great progress in this discipline will never be expected from the diverse pursuits of so many persons."[4]

III. Today more than ever the work of exegetes is needed, because many writings are being spread abroad in which the truth of the deeds and words which are contained in the Gospels is questioned. For this reason the Pontifical Biblical Commission, in pursuit of the task given to it by the Supreme Pontiffs, has considered it proper to set forth and insist upon the following points.

IV. 1. Let the Catholic exegete, following the guidance of the Church, derive profit from all that earlier interpreters, especially the holy Fathers and Doctors of the Church, have contributed to the understanding of the sacred text. And let him carry on their labors still further. **In order to put the abiding truth and authority of the Gospels in their full light, he will accurately adhere to the norms of rational and Catholic hermeneutics. He will diligently employ the new exegetical aids, above all those which the historical method, taken in its widest sense, offers to him — a method which carefully investigates sources and defines their nature and value, and makes use of such helps as textual criticism, literary criticism, and the study of languages. The interpreter will heed the advice of Pius XII of happy memory, who enjoined him "prudently ... to examine what contribution the manner of expression or the literary genre used by the sacred writer makes to a true and genuine** interpretation. **And let him be convinced that this part of his task cannot be neglected without serious detriment to Catholic exegesis.**"[5] By this piece of advice Pius XII of happy memory enunciated a general rule of hermeneutics by which the books of the Old Testament as well as the New must be explained. For in composing them the sacred writers employed the way of thinking and writing which was in vogue among their contemporaries. Finally, **the exegete will use all the means available to prove more deeply into the nature of Gospel testimony, into the religious life of the early churches, and into the sense and the value of apostolic tradition.**

V.   As occasion warrants, the interpreter may examine what reasonable elements are contained in the "form-critical method" that can be used for a fuller understanding of the Gospels. But let him be wary, because quite inadmissible philosophical and theological principles have often come to be mixed with this method, which not uncommonly have vitiated the method itself as well as the conclusions in the literary area. For some proponents of this method have been led astray by the prejudiced views of rationalism. They refuse to admit the existence of a supernatural order and the intervention of a personal God in the world through strict revelation, and the possibility and existence of miracles and prophecies. Others begin with a false idea of faith, as if it had nothing to do with historical truth — or rather were incompatible with it. Others deny the historical value and nature of the documents of revelation almost a priori. Finally, others make light of the authority of the apostles as witnesses to Christ, and of their task and influence in the primitive community, extolling rather the creative power of that community. All such views are not only opposed to Catholic doctrine, but are also devoid of scientific basis and alien to the correct principles of historical method.

VI. 2.   **To judge properly concerning the reliability of what is transmitted in the Gospels, the** interpreter should pay diligent attention to the three stages of tradition by which the doctrine and the life of Jesus have come down to us.

VII.   *Christ our Lord* joined to himself chosen disciples,[6] who followed him from the beginning,[7] saw his deeds, heard his words, and in this way were equipped to be witnesses of his life and doctrine.[8] When the Lord was orally explaining his doctrine, he followed the modes of reasoning and of exposition which were in vogue at the time. He accommodated himself to the mentality of his listeners and saw to it that what he taught was firmly impressed on the mind and easily remembered by the disciples. These people understood the miracles and other events of the life of Jesus correctly, as deeds performed or designed that human beings might believe in Christ through them, and embrace with faith the doctrine of salvation.

VIII.   *The apostles* proclaimed above all the death and resurrection of the Lord, as they bore witness to Jesus.[9] They faithfully explained his life and words,[10] while taking into account in their method of preaching the circumstances in which their listeners found themselves.[11] After Jesus rose from the dead and his divinity was clearly perceived,[12] faith, far from destroying the memory of what had transpired, rather confirmed it, because their faith rested on the things which Jesus did and taught.[13] Nor was he changed into a "mythical" person and his teaching deformed in consequence of the worship which the disciples from that time on paid Jesus as the Lord and the Son of God. On the other hand, there is no reason to deny that the apostles passed on to their listeners what was really said and done by the Lord with that fuller understanding which they enjoyed,[14] having been instructed by the glorious events of the Christ and taught by the light of the Spirit of Truth.[15] So, just as Jesus himself after his resurrection "interpreted to them"[16] the words of the Old Testament as well as his own,[17] they too interpreted his words and deeds according to the needs of their listeners. "Devoting themselves to the ministry of the word,"[18] they preached and made use of various modes of speaking which were suited to their own purpose and the mentality of their listeners. For they were debtors[19] "to Greeks and barbarians, to the wise and the foolish."[20] But these modes of speaking with which the preachers proclaimed Christ must be distinguished and (properly) assessed: catecheses, stories, testimonia, hymns, doxologies, prayers — and other literary forms of this sort which were in Sacred Scripture and were accustomed to be used by people of that time.

IX.   This primitive instruction, which was at first passed on by word of mouth and then in writing — for it soon happened that many tried "to compile a narrative of the things"[21] which concerned the Lord Jesus — was committed to writing by the sacred authors in four Gospels for the benefit of the churches, with a method suited to the peculiar purpose which each (author) set for himself. From the many things handed down they selected some things, reduced others to a synthesis, (still) others they explicated as they kept in mind the situation of the churches. With every (possible) means they sought that their reader might become aware of the reliability[22] of those words by which they had been instructed. Indeed, from what they had received the sacred writers above all selected the things which were suited to the various situations of the faithful and to the purpose which they had in mind, and adapted their narration of them to the same situations and purpose. Since the meaning of a statement also depends on the sequence, the evangelists, in passing on the words and deeds of our Savior, explained these now in one context, now in another, depending on (their) usefulness to the readers. Consequently, let the exegete seek out the meaning intended by the evangelist in narrating a saying or a deed in a certain way or in placing it in a certain context. For the truth

of the story is not at all affected by the fact that the evangelists relate the words and deeds of the Lord in a different order,[23] and express his sayings not literally but differently, while preserving (their) sense.[24] For, as St. Augustine says, "It is quite probable that each evangelist believed it to have been his duty to recount what he had to in that order in which it pleased God to suggest it to his memory — in those things at least in which the order, whether it be this or that, detracts in nothing from the truth and authority of the Gospel. But why the Holy Spirit, who apportions individually to each one as he wills,[25] and who therefore undoubtedly also governed and ruled the minds of the holy (writers) in recalling what they were to write because of the preeminent authority which the books were to enjoy, permitted one to compile his narrative in this way, and another in that, anyone with pious diligence may seek the reason and with divine aid will be able to find it."[26]

X.   Unless the exegete pays attention to all these things which pertain to the origin and composition of the Gospels and makes proper use of all the laudable achievements of recent research, he will not fulfill his task of probing into what the sacred writers intended and what they really said. From the results of the new investigations it is apparent that the doctrine and the life of Jesus were not simply reported for the sole purpose of being remembered, but were "preached" so as to offer the Church a basis of faith and of morals. The interpreter (then), by tirelessly scrutinizing the testimony of the evangelists, will be able to illustrate more profoundly the perennial theological value of the Gospels and bring out clearly how necessary and important the Church's interpretation is.

XI.   There are still many things, and of the greatest importance, in the discussion and explanation of which the Catholic exegete can and must freely exercise his skill and genius so that each may contribute his part to the advantage of all, to the continued progress of sacred doctrine, to the preparation and further support of the judgment to be exercised by the ecclesiastical magisterium, and to the defense and honor of the Church.[27] But let him always be disposed to obey the magisterium of the Church and not forget that the apostles, filled with the Holy Spirit, preached the good news, and that the Gospels were written under the inspiration of the Holy Spirit, who preserved their authors from error. "Now we have not learned of the plan of our salvation from any others than those through whom the Gospel has come to us. Indeed, what they once preached they later passed on to us in the Scriptures by the will of God, as the ground and pillar of our faith. It is not right to say that they preached before they had acquired perfect knowledge, as some would venture to say who boast of being correctors of the apostles. In fact, after our Lord rose from the dead and they were invested with power from on high, as the Holy Spirit came down upon them, they were filled with all (his gifts) and had perfect knowledge. They went forth to the ends of the earth, one and all with God's Gospel, announcing the news of God's bounty to us and proclaiming heavenly peace to men."[28]

XII. 3.   Those whose task it is to teach in seminaries and similar institutions should have it as their "prime concern that . . . Holy Scripture be so taught as both the dignity of the discipline and the needs of the times require."[29] Let teachers above all explain its theological teaching so that the Sacred Scriptures "may become for the future priests of the Church both a pure and never-failing source for their own spiritual life, as well as food and strength for the sacred task of preaching which they are about to undertake."[30] When they practice the art of criticism, especially so-called literary criticism, let them not pursue it as an end in itself, but that through it they might more plainly perceive the sense intended by God through the sacred writer. Let them not stop, therefore,

halfway, content only with their literary discoveries, but show in addition how these things really contribute to a clearer understanding of revealed doctrine, or if it be the case, to the refutation of errors. Instructors who follow these norms will enable their students to find in Sacred Scripture that which can "raise the mind to God, nourish the soul, and further the interior life."[31]

XIII. 4.   Those who instruct the Christian people in sacred sermons have need of great prudence. Let them above all pass on doctrine, mindful of St. Paul's warning: "Look to yourself and your teaching; hold on to that. For by so doing you will save both yourself and those who listen to you."[32] They are to refrain entirely from proposing idle or insufficiently established novelties. As for new opinions already solidly established, they may explain them, if need be, but with caution and due care for their listeners. When they narrate biblical events, let them not add imaginative details which are not consonant with the truth.

XIV.   This virtue of prudence should be cherished especially by those who publish for the faithful. Let them carefully bring forth the heavenly riches of the divine word "that the faithful . . . may be moved and inflamed rightly to conform their lives (to them)."[33] They should consider it a sacred duty never to depart in the slightest degree from the common doctrine and tradition of the Church. They should indeed exploit all the real advances of biblical science which the diligence of recent (students) has produced. But they are to avoid entirely the rash remarks of innovators.[34] They are strictly forbidden to disseminate, led on by some pernicious itch for novelty, any trial solutions for difficulties without a prudent selection and serious discrimination, for thus they disturb the faith of many.

XV.   This Pontifical Biblical Commission has already considered it proper to recall that books and articles in magazines and newspapers on biblical subjects are subject to the authority and jurisdiction of ordinaries, since they treat of religious matters and pertain to the religious instruction of the faithful.[35] Ordinaries are therefore requested to keep watch with great care over popular writings of this sort.

XVI. 5. Those who are in charge of biblical associations are to comply faithfully with the norms laid down by the Pontifical Biblical Commission.[36]

XVII.   If all these things are observed, the study of the Sacred Scriptures will contribute to the benefit of the faithful. Even in our time everyone realizes the wisdom of what St. Paul wrote: The sacred writings "can instruct (us) for salvation through faith in Christ Jesus. All Scripture is divinely inspired and profitable for teaching, for reproof, for correction, and for training in uprightness, so that the man of God may be perfect, equipped for every good work."[37]

XVIII.   The Holy Father, Pope Paul VI, at the audience graciously granted to the undersigned secretary on 21 April 1964, approved this Instruction and ordered the publication of it.

Rome, 21 April 1964
Secretary of the Commission
Benjamin N. Wambacq O. Praem.

NOTES

11.   Compare Acts 13:16-41 with Acts 17:22-31.
12.   Acts 2:36; John 20:28.
13.   Acts 2:22; 10:37-39.
14.   John 2:22; 12:16; 11:51-52; cf. 14:26; 16:12-13; 7:39.
15.   John 14:26; 16:13.
16.   Luke 24:27.
17.   Luke 24:44-45; Acts 1:3.
18.   Acts 6:4.
19.   1 Corinthians 9:19-23.
20.   Romans 1:14.
21.   Luke 1:1.
22.   Luke 1:4.
23.   See John Chrysostom, *Homilies on Matthew* 1,3 (PG 57, 16-17).
24.   Augustine, *De consensu evangelistarum,* 2.12,28 (PL 34. 1090-91; CSEL 43. 127-129).
25.   1 Corinthians 12:11.
26.   *De consensu evangelistarum* 2:21, 51-52 (PL 34. 1102; CSEL 43. 127-129).
27.   *Divino Afflante Spiritu,* #47.
28.   Irenaeus, *Against Heresies,* 3.1,1 (Harvey 2.2; PG 7.844).
29.   Apostolic Letter, *Quoniam in re biblica.*
30.   *Divino Afflante Spiritu,* #55.
31.   *Divino Afflante Spiritu,* # 25.
32.   1 Timothy 4:16.
33.   *Divino Afflante Spiritu,* # 50.
34.   Apostolic Letter, *Quoniam in re biblica,* 13.
35.   Instruction *De consociationibus biblicis.*
36.   Ibid.
37.   2 Timothy 3:15-17.

1.   1 Timothy 3:15.
2.   Pius XII, *Divino Afflante Spiritu* (1943), #47.
3.   See *Spiritus Paraclitus* 2,3 [AAS 12 (1920) 392].
4.   Apostolic Letter *Vigilantiae.*
5.   *Divino Afflante Spiritu,* # 38.
6.   Mark 3:14; Luke 6:13.
7.   Luke 1:2; Acts 1:21-22.
8.   Luke 24:28; John 15:27; Acts 1:8; 10:39; 13:31.
9.   Luke 24:44-48; Acts 2:32; 3:15; 5:30-32.
10.   Acts 10:36-41.

2. THE THREE STAGES OF THE COMPOSITION OF THE GOSPELS (VATICAN II)

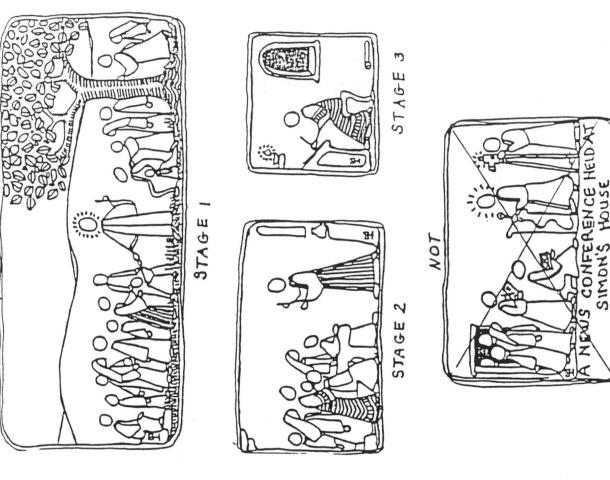

STAGE 1

STAGE 2

STAGE 3

NOT

A NEWS CONFERENCE HELD AT SIMON'S HOUSE

Mary E. Ingenthron

STAGE 1 "THE LIVED GOSPEL"

Holy Mother Church has firmly and with absolute constancy held, and continues to hold, that the four gospels just named, whose historical character the Church unhesitatingly asserts, faithfully hand on what Jesus Christ, while living among us, really did and taught for our eternal salvation until the day He was taken up into heaven (see Acts 1:1-2).

STAGE 2 "THE ORAL GOSPEL"

Indeed, after the ascension of the Lord the apostles handed on to their hearers what He had said and done. This they did with that clearer understanding which they enjoyed after they had been instructed by the events of Christ's risen life and taught by the light of the Spirit of truth.

STAGE 3 "THE WRITTEN GOSPELS"

The sacred authors wrote the four gospels, selecting some things from the many which had been handed on by word of mouth or in writing, reducing some of them to a synthesis, explaining some things in view of the situation of their churches, and preserving the form of proclamation but always in such a fashion that they told us the honest truth about Jesus. For their intention in writing was that either from their own memory and recollections, or from the witness of those who themselves "from the beginning were eyewitnesses and ministers of the word" we might know "the truth" concerning those matters about which we have been instructed (see Luke 1:2-4).

— from *The Dogmatic Constitution on Divine Revelation (Dei Verbum)*, #19

We must always remember these stages of composition for the gospels in order to interpret them correctly. If we understand what is described above about the process of composition, we will never confuse the gospels with eyewitness or earwitness recordings of the life and words of Jesus. The gospels are narrative proclamations of the good news of our salvation—the Christian gospel that Jesus of Nazareth lived, suffered, died and rose from the dead and this is indeed our salvation. This truth is the constant factor in every genuine Christian proclamation of the gospels no matter what form—living example, oral preaching, or written texts—that this message takes.

3. TRUTH AND ITS MANY EXPRESSIONS
VATICAN II ON HOW TO INTERPRET THE SCRIPTURES

Excerpts from *The Dogmatic Constitution on Divine Revelation (Dei Verbum)*

#10. Sacred tradition and sacred Scripture form one sacred deposit of the word of God, which is committed to the Church. Holding fast to this deposit, the entire holy people united with their shepherds remain always steadfast in the teaching of the apostles, in the common life, in the breaking of the bread, and in prayers, so that in holding to, practicing, and professing the heritage of the faith, there results on the part of the bishops and faithful a remarkable common effort.

The task of authentically interpreting the word of God, whether written or handed on, has been entrusted exclusively to the living teaching office of the Church, whose authority is exercised in the name of Jesus Christ. This teaching office is not above the word of God, but serves it, teaching only what has been handed on, listening to it devoutly, guarding it scrupulously, and explaining it faithfully by divine commission and with the help of the Holy Spirit; it draws from this one deposit of faith everything which it presents for belief as divinely revealed.

It is clear, therefore, that sacred tradition, sacred Scripture, and the teaching authority of the Church, in accord with God's most wise design, are so linked and joined together that one cannot stand without the others, and that all together and each in its own way under the action of the one Holy Spirit contribute effectively to the salvation of souls.

CHAPTER 3. SACRED SCRIPTURE: ITS DIVINE INSPIRATION AND ITS INTERPRETATION

#11. Those divinely revealed realities which are contained and presented in sacred Scripture have been committed to writing under the inspiration of the Holy Spirit. Holy Mother Church, relying on the belief of the apostles, holds that the books of both the Old and New Testament in their entirety, with all their parts, are sacred and canonical because, having been written under the inspiration of the Holy Spirit they have God as their author and have been handed on as such to the Church herself. In composing the sacred books, God chose men and while employed by God they made use of their powers and abilities, so that with God acting in them and through them, they, as true authors, consigned to writing everything and only those things which God wanted.

Therefore, since everything asserted by the inspired authors or sacred writers must be held to be asserted by the Holy Spirit, it follows that the books of Scripture must be acknowledged as teaching firmly, faithfully, and without error that truth which God wanted put into the sacred writings for the sake of our salvation. Therefore, "all Scripture is inspired by God and useful for teaching, for reproving, for correcting, for instruction in justice; that the man of God may be perfect, equipped for every good work" (2 Tim 3:16-17).

#12. However, since God speaks in sacred Scripture through men in human fashion, the interpreter of sacred Scripture, in order to see clearly what God wanted to communicate to us, should carefully investigate what **meaning** the sacred writers really intended, and what God wanted to manifest by means of their words.

Those who search out the intention of the sacred writers must, among other things, have regard for the **"literary forms."** For truth is proposed and expressed in a variety of ways, depending on whether a text is history of one kind or another, or whether its form is that of prophecy, poetry, or some other type of speech.

The interpreter must investigate what meaning the sacred writer intended to express and actually expressed in particular circumstances as he used contemporary literary forms in accordance with the **situation of his own time and culture.**

For the correct understanding of what the sacred author wanted to assert, due attention must be paid to the **customary and characteristic styles of perceiving, speaking, and narrating** which prevailed at the time of the sacred writer, and to the **customs people normally followed at that period** in their everyday dealings with one another.

But, since holy Scripture must be read and interpreted according to the same Spirit by whom it was written, no less serious attention must be given to the content and unity of the whole of Scripture, if the meaning of the sacred texts is to be correctly brought to light. The living tradition of the whole Church must be taken into account along with the harmony which exists between elements of the faith. It is the task of exegetes to work according to these rules toward a better understanding and explanation of the meaning of Sacred Scripture, so that through preparatory study the judgment of the Church may mature. For all of what has been said about the way of interpreting Scripture is subject finally to the judgment of the Church, which carries out the divine commission and ministry of guarding and interpreting the word of God.

AN APPLICATION OF #12 FOR OUR OWN SCRIPTURAL EXEGESIS

The goal of Scripture study is the understanding of **MEANING**, which demands locating a text within its contexts, moving beyond simple facts to also indicate their significance.

The first step recognizes the **LITERARY CONTEXT**. We must learn to read the texts according to the best methods of interpretation of literature, and in particular we must not confuse types of literature.

The second step recognizes the **HISTORICAL CONTEXT**. We must learn to interpret texts in their own historical time and in the specific situations in which they were composed.

The third step recognizes the **SOCIAL (CULTURAL) AND RHETORICAL CONTEXT**. We must learn to recognize the cultural situation out of which the texts came and for which they were a response in accord with the communication needs of the original audience.

For the full understanding [exegesis] of the meaning of a text, all of these methods must be used. But after our exegesis, we must finally make the **APPLICATION** of this meaning to our situation today. This application is essential, and can only be done well if we have considered as thoroughly as possible what the text meant to the original audience and in the living tradition of the Church community. We must also carefully examine our own presuppositions for applying the text.

4. THE SYNOPTIC SOURCES AND COMPARISONS

DIAGRAM OF THE GOSPEL SOURCES

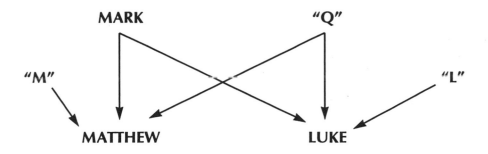

SYNOPTIC COMPARISONS

The Gospels of Mark, Matthew, and Luke are called synoptic because they can be "viewed together" and compared in parallel columns [as in your *Synopsis* book]. They reveal similarities because both Matthew and Luke had the written gospel of Mark as one of their sources. They both accepted much of Mark's material, yet they also edited it and added materials from their own respective community traditions (identified as "M" and "L" above) and from another common source ("Q" material).

GOSPEL	TOTAL VERSES	MARKAN MATERIAL	"Q" MATERIAL	SPECIAL MATERIAL
MARK	661	—	—	40
MATTHEW	1068	600	235	230
LUKE	1149	350	235	548

Of the verses Matthew does not use from Mark, Luke uses about 30 of them. Therefore, there are only about 25-30 verses in all of Mark which are not used somewhere in Matthew or Luke.

Not only is the substance of Mark reproduced, but often his very words are used. Matthew uses 51 percent of Mark's own words, while Luke uses 53 percent of them.

5. A HANDY GUIDE TO USING THE *GOSPEL PARALLELS*

To use your *Synopsis of the Four Gospels* (Gospel Parallels book) you should follow these steps.

1. **LOCATE THE PASSAGE TO BE STUDIED.**
   You need to familiarize yourself with the table of contents and learn how to find passages from each of the gospels.

2. **NOTICE THE CHANGES THAT LUKE AND MATTHEW MAKE TO MARK'S TEXT.**
   Our basic working presupposition is that both Matthew and Luke had and used Mark's written gospel. For some reason, they each decided not to copy Mark's text as it stands but to change it in some way.
   SOME SAMPLE CHANGES:
   1. LOCATION of the text in a new place in their gospel.
   2. ALTERATION of Mark's text in some way, e.g.:
      a) addition of words, phrases, or sentences
      b) omission of words, phrases, or sentences
      c) modification of text, e.g. changing vocabulary, grammar, etc.
      d) changing the order of events from Mark's order

3. **REFLECT ON SOME POSSIBLE REASONS FOR THESE EDITORIAL CHANGES.**
   The general reason for any changes was the desire of Luke and Matthew to make their gospel more appropriate for the needs of their communities. In general, their concerns can usually be identified as:
   1. **THEOLOGICAL CONCERNS:**
      Each evangelist has a particular way of explaining our relationship to God. Each has a particular emphasis or perspective for presenting the meaning of who God is, who Jesus is, what Christian discipleship means, what the Church is, how to pray, etc. Each evangelist felt free to adapt his source materials to express these views in his own way.
   2. **COMMUNITY CONCERNS:**
      Each evangelist structures and explains the gospel message for a particular community and its unique needs at the time of writing, e.g. its composition of Jewish and Gentile Christians, its relation to the social, political and cultural situations of both the Jewish and Hellenistic worlds, its mission and ministry, and the special problems the community might have applying the gospel message to their lives.

4. **DRAW SOME CONCLUSIONS ABOUT THEIR EDITING OF MARK'S TEXT.**
   Although the conclusions we arrive at are never completely certain because we can never get back into the minds of the evangelists to check out our findings, nevertheless our conclusions often help us appreciate the ways that each evangelist shapes his gospel to proclaim the Christian message to a particular community. This reflection on their work is a good preparation for our own task of adapting the gospel message for our own times without undue fear or anxiety.

In summary, then, the steps to follow are:
1. LOCATE THE PASSAGE.
2. NOTICE THE CHANGES.
3. REFLECT ON WHY THE CHANGES ARE MADE.
4. DRAW SOME CONCLUSIONS ABOUT REASONS FOR THE CHANGES.

6. AN OUTLINE OF MARK'S PASSION
[Mark 14:1–16:8]

I. THE ANOINTING AND LAST SUPPER (14:1-31)

A. Plotting, Anointing, Betrayal (14:1-11)
    1.   The Plot of the Chief Priests and Scribes   (14:1-2)
    2.   The Anointing   (14:3-9)
    3.   The Betrayal by Judas   (14.10-11)

B. Arrangements for the Passover Meal   (14:12-16)

C. The Last Supper (14:17-31)
    1.   Prediction of Judas' Betrayal   (14:17-21)
    2.   The Supper   (14:22-25)
    3.   Prediction of Peter's Denial   (14:26-31)

II. JESUS' PRAYER AND ARREST (14:32-52)

    1.   Gethsemane   (14:32-42)
    2.   Arrest   (14:43-52)

III. THE TRIALS OF JESUS (14:53-15:15)

A. The Trial Before the High Priest   (14:53-65)

B. Peter's Three Denials   (14:66-72)

C. The Trial Before Pilate   (15:1-15)

IV. THE CRUCIFIXION AND DEATH (15:16-47)

A. The Mockery by Roman Soldiers   (15:16-20)

B   The Crucifixion   (15:21-32)

C. The Death of Jesus   (15:33-41)

D. The Burial   (15:42-47)

V. THE EMPTY TOMB AND MESSAGE OF THE RESURRECTION (16:1-8)

7. THE GOSPEL ACCORDING TO MARK: OVERVIEW

Few commentaries were made of this gospel version before the 19th century. From the 19th century on, critics began to believe that they had found in MARK the first written gospel and the principal source of MATTHEW and LUKE.

AUTHORSHIP: According to the constant tradition of the early Church, the author was one Mark, the "interpreter of Peter." Some have wondered if he is the John-Mark we find in ACTS. We probably will never know for sure!

AUDIENCE: A mixed community of both Jewish and Gentile Christians (probably more Gentile Christians), located in an important Christian center, possibly Rome (but some scholars suggest Syria).

DATE: MARK is ordinarily dated from 65-70 A.D., at the time of the Roman Jewish war in Palestine (the destruction of the Jerusalem temple occurred in 70) and Roman persecution of Christians under the emperor Nero.

COMMUNITY SITUATION: The community is struggling with a genuine understanding of Christ and with their role as his disciples in a time of suffering and distress. It is a time of war, Roman persecution, martyrdom (e.g. of Peter and Paul), and a time of unrest within the community itself between the Jewish Christians and the Gentile Christians.

PURPOSE: To proclaim the Christian message in the form of ministry and passion of Jesus, and in the process re-orient the community's understanding of Jesus' messianic suffering and death and the demands of their own discipleship.

CHARACTERISTICS AND LITERARY STYLE:

MARK has a simple and direct style. He constantly engages the reader and challenges us to greater response. The pace of the gospel is extremely rapid and urgent. *Action* is the word here, as Jesus is a *doer* (much more than a *talker*) who is constantly on the move.

MARK emphasizes the humanity of Jesus:
> he has many emotions;
> he is subject to plots;
> he is misunderstood and even rejected by his own family and townspeople as well as the Jewish leaders;
> he suffers much;
> there are some things he does not know.

MARK also portrays the disciples as very human. Mark's portrait of the disciples stresses their failure rather than their virtues. Mark uses them as a negative example of discipleship. Since they do not really understand who Jesus is nor follow Jesus through his suffering to death, we can profit by their failure but we cannot do as they do.

MAJOR MARKAN THEMES:

Understanding/misunderstanding who Jesus is and what it means to be his disciples.

Openness to Gentiles.

Unity in community through the Eucharist.

Combat of Good and Evil.

Miracles as signs of Jesus' authority and of his ushering in the Kingdom of God.

God as Father (Abba) even in the midst of suffering.

Inside/Outside (those who believe and those who do not).

MARK'S PORTRAIT OF JESUS:

CHRIST/MESSIAH:
> 1:1; 8:29; 14:61 (climax of first part of the gospel is Peter's confession in 8:29, after which Jesus gives his identity as Messiah in terms of suffering, death, resurrection).

SON OF GOD:
> 1:1,11; 3:11; 5:7; 9:7; 14:61; 15:39.

SON OF MAN:
> 2:10 (forgive sins);
> 2:38 (authority over Sabbath);
> 8:31; 9:9; 9:12; 9:31; 10:33; 10:45; 14:21 (must suffer, be delivered up);
> 8:38; 13:26; 14:62 (will come).

SUFFERING SERVANT:
> (throughout, especially in "Prediction Passages" and the passion narrative — how Jesus is Messiah)

MIRACLE WORKER AND TEACHER:
> (chapters 1–8)

BUILDER OF THE KINGDOM COMMUNITY:
> (chapters 5–8)

LAWGIVER FOR THE KINGDOM COMMUNITY:
> (chapter 7)

MARK'S PORTRAIT OF DISCIPLESHIP:

Conversion (1:15 — faith in the Good News)

Total response to call of the Lord; leave behind all that would keep one from following Jesus.

Called to "be with" Jesus, and to be sent out to preach and have authority over demons (3:14-15)

Follow Jesus "on the way" (carry cross; service; deny self; give life for others; be like little children)

WHAT HAPPENS WITH THE DISCIPLES IN MARK:

misunderstanding; hardened hearts; abandon Jesus; weakness and failure; yet always children of the Father called to share in the life of Jesus.

GOSPEL PATTERN:

The pattern is the same for preparation (as seen in John the Baptist); fulfillment (as seen in Jesus); and realization (as seen in the Christian disciple) of the Kingdom of God:

TO PREACH,
TO BE DELIVERED UP,
TO SUFFER DEATH

8. COMMON MATERIAL IN THE INFANCY NARRATIVES

		MATTHEW	LUKE
1.	Mary is explicitly referred to as a virgin (Gk. *parthenos*)	1:23	1:27
2.	Jesus' parents, Mary and Joseph, are described as engaged, then married, but without marital intercourse	1:18,25	1:27,34
3.	Jesus is descended from the Davidic family	1:16,20	1:27,32
4.	An angel tells of the conception and future birth of Jesus	1:20-23	1:30-35
5.	Joseph plays no role in the conception of Jesus	1:20,23,25	1:34
6.	The role of the Holy Spirit in the conception of Jesus is explicitly referred to	1:18,20	1:35
7.	The name of Jesus is designated by God via the angel	1:21	1:31
8.	Jesus is regarded as savior	1:21	2:11
9.	Jesus' birth takes place after the parents are living together	1:24-25	2:5-6
10.	Jesus' birth takes place in the days of Herod the Great	2:1	1:5
11.	Jesus' birth takes place in Bethlehem of Judea	2:1	2:4-6
12.	The child Jesus grows up in Nazareth	2:23	2:3

9. HOW TO READ THE NATIVITY STORIES OF JESUS

By Macrina Scott, O.S.F.

As Christmas draws near, our hearts are filled with sacred pictures: the Virgin Mother dressed in blue, St. Joseph with white beard and brown cloak, the Wise Men in velvet and crowns leading camels, white-robed angels flying above the stable.

Someone with a scientific mentality could question us on every point. Can you prove that angels have wings? Or that Mary always wore blue?

Of course we can't, but we wouldn't think much of the intelligence of the one who asked the question. Anyone with common sense knows those things don't matter. We believe that our Creator has become one of us. This mystery is far beyond our understanding, yet we believe it and rejoice with all our hearts. At Christmastime, we celebrate it. In order to grasp the incarnation in some way, to allow it to be real to us, we need to picture it somehow.

We know that the mystery of the Nativity can be pictured in many ways. Occasionally we see it painted by a Chinese artist and all the figures have Oriental faces with slanted eyes. The picture implies that Jesus came to save the Chinese as well as the rest of the world, and we do not accuse the artist of misrepresenting the scene, because we know that the basic statement is true. A Swedish painter may show a blond mother and child in a Scandinavian farmhouse, and we accept that, too.

We are willing to allow artists a great deal of liberty in painting this most sacred of events, because we know that their purpose is to help us understand the mystery more deeply. Sometimes we fail to realize that the very first artists who painted the Nativity scene for us were Matthew and Luke, and that they are entitled to that same liberty, and for that same purpose.

The Artistry of Matthew and Luke

When St. Peter preached the Good News of Jesus, or when St. Mark wrote it down for the first time in the form of a written Gospel, the story did not begin with the birth of Christ at all. For Mark, it began with the opening of Jesus' public life, his baptism by John the Baptist. Mark's Gospel, considered to be the first Gospel written down, dealt with what eyewitnesses remembered of what Jesus did and said, how he suffered and died, and appeared again after his resurrection. That was all the first Christian converts knew, and it was enough.

But some years later when Matthew and Luke, quite independently of each other, felt dissatisfied with the simple Gospel of Mark and were inspired to try to improve on it, they added various things. To start, each of them added a kind of preface before the baptism of Jesus by John. Those prefaces we call the infancy narratives. They deal with the life of Jesus before he was 30 — or, rather, they appear to deal with that.

In reality, their significance goes much deeper. Like the artists who paint the Nativity today, Matthew and Luke were really trying to tell us something about the unfathomable mystery of the Incarnation — not about what Jesus did or how he looked, but about who he was and the significance of his coming among us. They are *theological* prefaces, written to show us how to interpret the events of the Gospel proper.

Unlike the main part of the Gospel, these prefaces were probably not based on eyewitness accounts. Matthew and Luke could talk with people still alive who had witnessed the actions and heard the words of the adult Jesus, but few, if any, were available who had witnessed the intimate scenes of his childhood.

Matthew and Luke did not see the lack of data about the baby Jesus as a problem. If they had had hospital records of the hour of his delivery, weight at birth and attending physician, they would not have thought such facts worthy of recording in their Gospels. Their concerns were much deeper. They wrote to nourish the faith of their readers, not to supply them with facts useful for a quiz show.

The Gospel writers were like the Chinese artist who doesn't bother to research what a first-century Jew might have looked like, but prefers to disregard those facts and paint Jesus and Mary as Chinese in order to express a message.

In the past, when scholars presumed the infancy narratives were factual accounts, like the rest of the Gospels, they had great difficulty showing how two versions of the events as different as Matthew's and Luke's could possibly both be true. We are so used to combining the two stories in our minds and in our pictures it is hard for us to read either one for what it really says. Yet examining these two accounts, and picking out the contrasts, can lead to greater appreciation of the Incarnation and deepening of our faith.

Two Different Stories

For Matthew, the child is born in a house in Bethlehem, which seems to be his parents' home. Nazareth is not mentioned until after their return from Egypt as a place to which Joseph brought his family to avoid Archelaus, son of Herod, who had massacred the children of Bethlehem in his search for Jesus. Luke says not a word about Egypt or the massacre, but begins his story with Mary living in Nazareth at the time of the Annunciation. The story of the census explains their being in Bethlehem.

For Luke, the Holy Family remains in Bethlehem only 40 days till the time for Mary's Purification, after which they return to Nazareth. Matthew shows them still in Bethlehem two years after the child's birth when the Magi arrive from the East.

In Luke, the Annunciation of the birth of Jesus is made to Mary. Matthew, who seems to show less interest in women than Luke does, describes the Annunciation as made to Joseph. Luke tells us of Mary's visit to her saintly relative Elizabeth, and of the prophetess Anna, neither of whom is mentioned by Matthew.

The differences could be multiplied indefinitely. If you read the two accounts completely separately, you will see for yourself what different stories they tell.

But these differences should not be seen as problems to be resolved, any more than differences between two paintings of the Nativity are problems. Each has its own beauty, its own message. Both are true on the level on which they are written — as expressions of deep theological realities. Probably neither is true in every detail in the way in which a hospital record is true. That is not the kind of truth the authors seek to express.

Matthew and Luke each had special aspects of the mystery of Jesus which he wanted to bring out in his Gospel, and each composes his preface to prepare his readers for what is coming, to clue them in to his principal themes.

Matthew—Voice of the Jews

Matthew is writing for Jewish Christians and for Gentiles who have recently joined them. For the Jewish Christians, the Old Testament is very sacred; it has molded their spiritual life from childhood. Matthew is a good rabbi, and he teaches his Jewish Christians in the same way every rabbi taught his flock, centering everything on certain passages of the Old Testament. His goal is to reassure his readers that they have not lost their heritage as Jews: Jesus is the fulfillment of everything in the Jewish Scriptures. Matthew's most typical phrase, in the infancy narrative as throughout his Gospel, is, "And this happened in order to fulfill what was written in the prophets," followed by an Old Testament quotation. He seems to choose the stories he does because they happen to fit in well with the passages he wants to use from the Old Testament.

Matthew's whole account of the infancy of Jesus is modeled on the Old Testament story about the baby Moses. Jesus escaped the slaughter of the innocents, as Moses in the basket escaped the slaughter of the baby boys by Pharaoh. Matthew is telling his readers, for whom Moses is the greatest of religious leaders, that Jesus is the new Moses, like the one they knew but even greater.

Matthew's text hints that his Jewish Christian readers around 80 A.D. were living through a terrible crisis. They had accepted Jesus as the Jewish Messiah their people had been expecting, and they had thought that gradually all Jews would come to recognize him as such. But quite the opposite had happened. Many Jews, and particularly the religious leaders among them, the Pharisees, had become more and more threatened by the new movement, and had finally hardened their opposition to it to such an extent that they had excommunicated all Jews who followed Jesus from the synagogue and from all participation in the Jewish community life. The Jewish Christians were rejected by family and friends as well as by their former religious leaders.

What astonished them even more was the fact that many Gentiles had accepted Jesus as the Messiah. Their whole world had turned topsy-turvy.

Jesus' Persecution Mirrors That of Jewish Christians

So Matthew comforted them with a story which said it was not just they who were rejected by their leaders and neighbors, but Jesus himself. So he shows Jesus born in the Jewish town of Bethlehem, but he does not mention the shepherds, Elizabeth and Zechariah, Anna and Simeon, or any other Jew as welcoming him. Only the Gentile Magi come from far away to worship. And when they do come, the Jewish king and the Sanhedrin (the council of Jewish religious leaders) oppose and try to kill Jesus, in the process making martyrs

of those Jews who are somehow connected with him. The Innocents must have seemed to the Jewish Christians of 80 A.D. a symbol of what they feared would happen to them. Then Matthew shows Jesus, threatened with death in the land of the Jews, fleeing for safety to Gentile Egypt.

The whole mood of Matthew's infancy narrative matches the mood of the sad and frightened Jewish Christians who were living through the terrible disillusionment of seeing their religious leaders turn finally against Jesus and against themselves.

The story begins with a respectable Jew, Joseph, who has discovered that his fiancée is pregnant with a child that is not his, and is thrown into a very human consternation. The Son of God has taken on human flesh, but his arrival is not greeted with enthusiasm by the first Jewish man who knew of it. After an angel assures Joseph, however, that Mary has conceived through the power of the Holy Spirit, he quite willingly accepts her as his wife.

The next Jew to hear of the coming of Christ, King Herod, was filled with jealousy and anger, and the Sanhedrin and all Jerusalem, says Matthew, were troubled as well. If we looked on these stories as literal history we would have a hard time believing them. The Jewish people hated Herod, and it is impossible to imagine that all the Jews living in Jerusalem shared his insane jealousy of a newborn baby who might be the Messiah for whom they were hoping. But Matthew is expressing the feelings of the early Jewish Christians that all Jews had gathered forces against them.

Next, Matthew tells of the flight into Egypt and the gruesome story of the slaughter of the Innocents, and the weeping and wailing of their mothers. There is not much jolly Christmas spirit in Matthew's story. In fact, there is only one ray of light in the whole picture — the Magi, guided to Jesus by their star and rejoicing as they worship him. Everything else is dark, full of consternation and anger, violence and fear.

That is the Christmas story as Matthew tells it. I think we can gain very much from meditating over it, especially in times of suffering. Like the Passion story later in the Gospel, it helps us realize that Jesus experienced rejection and pain and is able to be with us and understand us in our trials.

How the Infancy Narratives Arose

The Infancy Gospels, which apparently arose only in certain areas of the primitive Church, were intended to be theological expansions of the bare data contained in the memory of the early life of Jesus by the use of the Old Testament and of the developed belief in his divine sonship and his Messiahship. Thus the infancy narratives are proclamations of his supernatural origin and character and anticipations of the revelation of him as Messiah and Lord to both Jews and Gentiles. In Matthew the revelation meets with profound hostility; Luke does not exhibit this element. In both Matthew and Luke the infancy anticipates the passion and death of Jesus.

Such freedom in handling the material is in harmony with the purpose of the Gospels as a proclamation of faith, and with the characteristic literary feature of the Gospels by which they adapt the traditions to the belief of the Church which they set forth.

John L. McKenzie, S.J.
Dictionary of the Bible

Luke—Voice of the Gentiles

The mood and message of Luke's infancy narrative are very different, as is the story he tells. He never mentions Joseph's embarrassment over Mary's pregnancy, the slaughter of the Innocents or the flight into Egypt.

Luke's is the story we usually think of as we meditate on the mysteries of the rosary, or prepare for the celebration of Christmas. It is the good news that a savior has been born for *all* people. Luke is a Gentile, writing for mainly Gentile readers, who are hardly aware of the crisis through which the Jewish Christians are going. These Gentiles are only aware that Jesus was a Jew, and that they themselves have received the wonderful news of salvation only because of the Jews who had raised Jesus, supported him during his public ministry and formed the very first generation of the Church, which had sent out missionaries to the Gentiles. So Luke wants to teach them to look back with reverent gratitude to the Jewish people. (His message is for us Gentiles today, also.)

All the Jews in his infancy narrative are beautiful, Spirit-filled people, eagerly expecting the Messiah and welcoming him with love and joy. He tells us of Zechariah and Elizabeth, Simeon and Anna, the shepherds and the Jewish doctors who gathered in admiration around Jesus when he was 12 years old.

It is Luke who tells us of Mary. Matthew, and probably most of his Jewish Christian readers, lived in a man's world in which woman's main role was to bear children. But from Luke we learn what Catholic tradition has always emphasized — that Mary's greatness does not come so much from the physical fact of her motherhood as from her spiritual greatness. Luke is emphasizing Mary, as he emphasizes women throughout his Gospel, not because he thinks what happened when Jesus was a baby particularly important, but because he wants to highlight the importance of women in the Church for all time.

Luke also stresses prayer throughout his Gospel. He often shows Jesus at prayer. And in the infancy narratives, he alone gives us the great New Testament canticles, such as those uttered by Zechariah, Mary and Simeon — not to mention the angels' song on Christmas night.

Luke Accents Jesus' Poverty

Another special interest of Luke's is the poverty of Christ, and the poverty to which the Christian is called. Matthew tells us nothing of the poverty of Jesus' birth, but shows Jesus to us in a house receiving the homage of wealthy and important travelers from far away, bringing him very expensive gifts.

Only Luke tells the story of Mary and Joseph — like the poor throughout the centuries — having their lives disrupted by the whim of the powerful who want a census of their subjects. So when Jesus is born he does not even have a home of his own, but is given temporary lodging in a stable. There is no bed for him, so he is laid in the animals' manger. Luke is preparing us for the words of Jesus he will report later in his Gospel: "The foxes have holes, and the birds of the air have nests, but the Son of Man has nowhere to rest his head." Only the shepherds — a poor and despised class — come to honor the child in Luke's Gospel.

Later, in telling of Mary's Purification, Luke tells us that she offered two turtledoves — an offering the poor were permitted to make instead of the usual lamb. Again, he is reminding us that Jesus was born into a poor family. Matthew mentions neither manger nor shepherds nor Mary's Purification. Luke does mention these details, not because he thinks it important in what kind of building Jesus was born, or in what kind of crib he was laid, but to make vivid for us the reality that the Son of God chose to come among us as a poor man.

Matthew and Luke — Their Underlying Message

It becomes clear that Matthew and Luke paint in words two very different pictures of the birth and early life of Jesus. If we were dealing with human historical documents, we might ask, "Which is true and which is false?" But when we are dealing with the Word of God, we know that neither can be false.

In the past, Catholic authors went through all kinds of intellectual gymnastics to show that there really was no contradiction where common sense said that, indeed, there was a contradiction. But Pope Pius XII freed them, and us, to use our intelligence in more fruitful ways when he pointed out in his encyclical *Divino Afflante Spiritu* that scholars must search out the literary form in which each part of Scripture was written. He admonished scholars to search among the literary remains contemporary with the Bible to find out what was expected of an author in those ancient times.

One thing we have learned about the ancient authors is that they were much less insistent than we are on scientific or historical facts. They were more interested in the meaning of things, the underlying message. And it was considered quite appropriate for an author to write, for instance, an account of the infancy of a great man without having any actual information about it. The writer knew the man as an adult, and therefore felt certain that he had been born and had a father and mother. The author was then free to invent the other details in such a way as to point to the kind of person the man did in fact become.

True Portraits of Jesus

So Matthew and Luke may have known little about the facts of Jesus' babyhood, but they felt justified in creating any incidents which would point out what kind of man Jesus was to be: that he was the Messiah awaited by the Jews, but rejected by most of them; a king and savior of all; one who identified with the poor and lifted woman to her true dignity; and so forth.

Rather than being preoccupied with the historical accuracy of the accounts, we must try to grasp these truths about Jesus. Once we understand Matthew's and Luke's perspectives, we can only say that the pictures painted so differently by them are both profoundly true.

10. THE ANNUNCIATION PATTERN

Scholars have noticed the similarities between the story of the annunciation to Mary with that of several annunciations in the Old Testament. These stories very probably served as the model for the Lucan use and development of this pattern in his gospel. The pattern is stereotyped and helps orient the reader to important aspects of the career of the person in salvation history. The stages of the pattern are:

1. The *appearance* of an angel of the Lord or the Lord in person:
   — Zechariah (Lk:1:11), Mary (Lk 1:26-27), shepherds (Lk 2:9)
   — Joseph (Mt 1:20), Abraham (Gen 17:1), Samson's parents (Jgs 13:3,9,11)
   — Moses (Ex 3:2), Gideon (Jgs 6:11-12)

2. A *reaction* of fear, countered (sometimes) by "Do not be afraid":
   — Zechariah (Lk 1:12-13), Mary (Lk 1:29-30), shepherds (Lk 2:9-10)
   — Joseph (Mt 1:20), Abraham (Gen 17:3), Samson's parents (Jgs 13:6,22)
   — Moses (Ex 3:6), Gideon (Jgs 6:22-23)

3. An *announcement* about the birth of a son:
   a. Address by name or title:
      — Zechariah (Lk 1:13), Mary (Lk 1:28,30)
      — Joseph (Mt 1:20), Abraham (Gen 17:5)
      — Moses (Ex 3:4), Gideon (Jgs 6:12)

   b. The woman has conceived/will conceive and bear a son:
      — Zechariah (Lk 1:13), Mary (Lk 1:31), shepherds (Lk 2:11)
      — Joseph (Mt 1:20-21), Abraham (Gen 17:16, 19), Samson's parents (Jgs 13:3)

   c. The naming of the child (with etymology):
      — Zechariah (Lk 1:13), Mary (Lk 1:31)
      — Joseph (Mt 1:21), Abraham (Gen 17:19)

   d. The future accomplishments of this child:
      — Zechariah (Lk 1:15-17), Mary (Lk 1:32-33, 35), shepherds (Lk 2:11)
      — Joseph (Mt 1:21), Abraham (Gen 17:19), Samson's parents (Jgs 13:5)
      — Moses (Ex 3:10), Gideon (Jgs 6:14)

4. An *objection* from the person receiving the announcement:
   — Zechariah (Lk 1:18), Mary (Lk 1:34)
   — Abraham (Gen 17:17), Samson's parents (Jgs 13:17)
   — Moses (Ex 3:11), Gideon (Jgs 6:15)

5. The giving of a *sign* to reassure the recipient:
   — Zechariah (Lk 1:20), Mary (Lk 1:36-37), shepherds (Lk 2:12)
   — Samson's parents (Jgs 13:9, 18-21)
   — Moses (Ex 3:12), Gideon (Jgs 6:19-22)

11. PASSAGES UNIQUE TO LUKE'S GOSPEL — "L" PASSAGES

1:5–2:52	The infancy narrative
3:10-14	Preaching of John the Baptizer
3:23-38	The genealogy of Jesus
4:17-21,23,25-30	Jesus' visit to Nazareth
5:4-9	The catch of fish
5:39	Old wine and new wine
7:12-17	Raising the son of the widow of Nain
8:1-3	Galilean women as followers of Jesus

——————— LUKE'S MAJOR ADDITION TO MARK: THE JOURNEY SECTION ———————

9:52-55	Jesus' departure for Jerusalem and the Samaritan inhospitality
9:61-62	Farewell of a would-be follower
10:17 20	Return of the 72 disciples
10:25-28	Commandment for eternal life
10:29-37	Parable of the Good Samaritan
10:38-42	Martha and Mary
11:1	Setting for the "Our Father" prayer
11:5-8	Parable of the persistent friend
11:27-28	Those who are truly blessed
12:1	The leaven of the Pharisees
12:13-15	Warning against greed
12:16-21	Parable of the rich fool
12:35-38	Vigilance
12:47-48	The servant's reward
12:49	Jesus' mission
12:54-56	Signs of the times
13:1-9	Timely reform: parable of the barren fig tree
13:10-17	Cure of the crippled woman on the Sabbath
13:31-33	Herod's desire to kill Jesus; His departure from Galilee
14:1-6	Cure of the man with dropsy
14:7-14	Sayings on the proper conduct at dinners
14:28-32	Conditions of discipleship
15:8-10	Parable of the lost coin
15:11-32	Parable of the lost son [the prodigal]
16:1-8a	Parable of the dishonest manager
16:8b-12	Two applications of the parable
16:14-15	Reproof of the greedy Pharisees
16:19-31	Parable of the rich man and Lazarus
17:7-10	Unprofitable servants
17:12-19	Cleansing of the ten lepers
17:20-21	Coming of God's Kingdom
17:28-32	Days of the Son of Man
18:1-8	Parable of the dishonest judge
18:9-14	Parable of the Pharisee and the toll-collector
19:1-10	Zaccheus

——————— JESUS IN JERUSALEM ———————

19:39-40	Answer to the Pharisees
19:41-44	Lament over Jerusalem
20:18	Strength of stone
21:18,21b,22,24	Destruction of Jerusalem
21:34-36	Vigilance
21:37-38	Ministry of Jesus in Jerusalem
22:15-18,19c-20	The last supper
22:27	Who is greater, the one who dines or who serves?
22:31-32	Peter's denial foretold
22:35-38	The two swords
22:63-71	Mistreatment and interrogation of Jesus
23:6-12	Jesus sent to Herod (Herod's judgment)
23:13-16	Pilate's judgment
23:27-32	On the road to the cross
23:35a,36-37	Witnesses at the crucifixion
23:39b-43	Jesus' dialogue with the good thief
23:46,47b-49	The death of Jesus
23:56	Women preparing spices before the Sabbath
24:13-35	Jesus' appearance on the road to Emmaus
24:36-43	Jesus' appearance to the disciples in Jerusalem
24:44-49	Jesus' final commission

12. THE GOSPEL ACCORDING TO LUKE: OVERVIEW

AUTHORSHIP: The constant tradition of the early Church attributes the third gospel to a certain Luke described as a physician and companion of Paul. (cf. COLOSSIANS 4:14; PHILEMON 24; 2 TIMOTHY 4:11). While a few continue to maintain this tradition, there is a greater number of modern scholars who feel we simply cannot be sure. If the Luke mentioned above is not the author of the third gospel, then the evangelist's identity is simply not known.

AUDIENCE: A primarily Gentile Christian community possibly located at Antioch in Syria.

DATE: The date given by most scholars is between 75 and 90 A.D.
(Some 45-60 years after the death and resurrection of Jesus)

COMMUNITY SITUATION: The community is struggling with its role in a Gentile world. It faces serious questions concerning Gentiles following a faith based largely on Judaism. Were the missionaries who brought the message to this community reliable? How could the words of a Jewish rabbi (one Jesus who was crucified as a criminal) spoken to a Jewish audience a half century earlier be appropriate for a modern Gentile audience?
Luke will want his readers to know there is continuity with Jesus and the early Hebrew community, and that Gentiles were included in God's plan from the beginning even though the Jews were historically the first to hear the message as a channel for all others.

PURPOSE: To provide an authoritative account of the history of salvation as revealed in the OT fulfillment in the life and ministry of Jesus; which in turn serves as the foundation and pattern for the ministry and mission of the Church (presented in Luke's second volume, ACTS).
Luke provides a salvation history in terms of a journey with Jesus under the guidance of the Holy Spirit. This salvation history is composed of three periods:
1) **Promise:** (Time of Israel— preparation to receive Jesus as Messiah)
2) **Time of Jesus:** (Jesus' ministry, closing formally with the ascension)
3) **Time of the Church:** (continues ministry/mission of Jesus to the end of the world)

CHARACTERISTICS AND LITERARY STYLE:

LUKE demonstrates literary excellence and a profound understanding of Greek literary structure. This gospel is very well written and exhibits a rich vocabulary (considered as representing the best Greek in the New Testament). LUKE/ACTS should be seen as one work (these works were in fact joined in the scriptures until JOHN was inserted between them).

In LUKE/ACTS the journey is a very important theme:

In LUKE,
> the journey is from Galilee to Jerusalem.

In ACTS,
> the journey is from Jerusalem to Rome.

MAJOR LUKAN THEMES:

Salvation (history of salvation; forgiveness of sins; related to physical healing)

Right use of wealth

Table fellowship with all (rich/poor, Gentile/Jew, men/women)

Universal mission (salvation of all; gospel of reconciliation and mercy; gospel of poor and lowly, sick, outcasts, Samaritans, tax collectors, women)

Peace/Prayer/Praise/Joy as a Christian response to God's salvation

The role of the Holy Spirit in directing God's plan

Christian life as a journey with Jesus

The Temple in Jerusalem

The twelve Apostles

LUKE'S PORTRAIT OF JESUS:

PROPHET: 1:76; 4:24; 7:16,39; 13:33; 22:64; 24:19

SAVIOR: 2:11; 19:10 — forgiveness of sins — 5:24; 7:48

MESSIAH: (who suffers) 2:11; 4:41; 9:20; 22:66; 24:26,46

SON OF MAN: 5:24 (forgives sins)
             6:5 (Lord of Sabbath)
             7:34 (ate and drank)
             9:22 (must suffer)
             9:44 (delivered up)
             9:58 (nowhere to lay his head)
            11:30 (sign to present age)
            12:40 (will come in glory)
            18:31 (must suffer)
            22:48 (betrayed by kiss)
             24:7 (delivered up)

FRIEND OF SINNERS / OUTCASTS:
            5:27-32 (Levi)
            7:29-35 (tax collectors)
            7:36-50 (Simon the Pharisee)
            8:1-3 (women)
            15:1f (tax collectors, etc.)

LUKE'S PORTRAIT OF DISCIPLESHIP:

Note the story of Zaccheus as an example:
> tax collector invited by Jesus; small in stature; wealthy;
> eager to see Jesus; welcomes Jesus; table fellowship;
> defends self vs. accusers/innocence as "sinner";
> generous to poor; more than just in business;
> genuine child of Abraham because of above attitudes;
> salvation comes to him in the person of Jesus.

GOSPEL PATTERN (OF LUKE AND ACTS ALSO):

Jesus and his message are
> REVEALED -
> PROCLAIMED -

SOME ACCEPT - (positive response)

SOME REJECT - (negative response)

13. A Chronology of the Events of Holy Week

Sunday	Monday	Tuesday	Wednesday	Thursday	Friday	Sat.	Sun.
Entrance with Palms (Bethany to Bethpage)	Warning to the Fig Tree	Withered Fig Tree	(T) Silent in Bethany	(T) Silent in Bethany	(E - early) Pilate (2) Scourging Via Dolorosa		"first light" women go to tomb to complete anointing of body
money changers	Temple	Temple	(E) Caiphas?	(E) Sanhedrin (does not break 24-hour trial law)	9:00 A.M. — Crucifixion		
temple teaching	Returns to Bethany	Last Public Discourse (Mt 23)	Jesus under Arrest	(E - P.M.) Pilate (1) Herod Antipas	12 noon — Darkness		
Returns to Bethany		Olivet Discourse (Little Apocalypse Mt 24)		(time for Pilate's wife to have a dream)	3:00 P.M. — Death		
Feast at Simon, the Leper's house		(E) Last Supper		(T) Last Supper	entombment completed by sunset		
		(E) Garden		(T) *see list of events on next page*			
		(E) Annas					
		(E) Caiphas?					

Explanation of Above Chart

The chart above shows two alternate chronologies for the events of Holy Week.

    (T) indicates the events according to the traditional calendar, while

    (E) situates the events in light of the Essene calendar.

With the traditional schedule of events, there is the difficulty of fitting in all the events mentioned below following the Thursday Last Supper but before the 9:00 A.M. crucifixion time.

If the Last Supper is on Thursday night, where do you fit the following:

Four hours for the Passover

New Covenant (Eucharist)

Going to Gethsemane

Three late night prayer meetings

Judas to Garden

Arrest

Six trials:

    Annas (reigning dynasty)

    Caiphas (current high priest)

    Sanhedrin (early A.M.)

    Pilate

    Herod Antipas (Luke only)

    Pilate (negotiate over Barabbas)

Scourging

Via Dolorosa

14. AN OUTLINE OF LUKE'S PASSION
[Luke 22:1–24:53]

I. THE PRELIMINARY EVENTS

1.	The Conspiracy of the Leaders	(22:1-2)
2.	The Betrayal of Jesus by Judas	(22:3-6)
3.	Preparation for the Passover Meal	(22:7-14)
4.	The Last Supper (Eucharist)	(22:15-20)
5.	Jesus Foretells His Betrayal	(22:21-23)
6.	Jesus' Remarks: Disciples and Their Places in the Kingdom	(22:24-30)
7.	Peter's Denial Foretold	(22:31-34)
8.	The Two Swords	(22:35-38)

II. THE PASSION, DEATH, AND BURIAL OF JESUS

9.	Prayer on the Mount of Olives	(22:39-46)
10.	The Arrest of Jesus	(22:47-53)
11.	Peter's Denials; Jesus before the Council	(22:54-71)
12.	Jesus Is Delivered to Pilate; the Trial	(23:1-5)
13.	Jesus Is Sent to Herod	(23:6-12)
14.	Pilate's Judgment	(23:13-16)
15.	Jesus Is Handed Over To Be Crucified	(23:18-25)
16.	The Road to the Cross	(23:26-32)
17.	The Crucifixion	(23:33-38)
18.	The Two Criminals	(23:39-43)
19.	The Death of Jesus	(23:44-49)
20.	The Burial of Jesus	(23:50-56a)

III. THE RESURRECTION NARRATIVE

21.	The Women at the Empty Tomb	(23:56b–24:12)
22.	Jesus Appears on the Road to Emmaus	(24:13-35)
23.	Jesus Appears to the Disciples in Jerusalem	(24:36-43)
24.	Jesus' Final Commission	(24:44-49)
25.	The Ascension	(24:50-53)

15. SELF-QUIZ ON MARK AND LUKE

MARK

1.   **WHEN** was the gospel of MARK written?
2.   **WHO** was Mark's original audience?
3.   **WHERE** was this audience located?
4.   **WHAT** was the situation in which Mark's community found themselves?
5.   **WHAT** was the evangelist's original purpose in writing this book?
6.   What do you consider to be the TWO most important themes in this book?
     1.
     2.
7.   How would you characterize the portrait of Jesus in Mark?
8.   How would you describe Mark's understanding of "genuine discipleship"?
9.   What is the most significant thing you have learned from this book?

LUKE

1.   **WHEN** was the gospel of LUKE written?
2.   **WHO** was Luke's original audience?
3.   **WHERE** was this audience located?
4.   **WHAT** was the situation in which Luke's community found themselves?
5.   **WHAT** was the evangelist's original purpose in writing this book?
6.   What do you consider to be the TWO most important themes in this book?
     1.
     2.
7.   How would you characterize the portrait of Jesus in Luke?
8.   How would you describe Luke's understanding of "genuine discipleship"?
9.   What is the most significant thing you have learned from this book?

OTHER INFORMATION

1)   Identify the three stages of gospel formation according to Vatican II.
2)   Which are the "synoptic" gospels? Why would they be called this?
3)   What is the "Q" source? How is it related to each of the synoptic gospels?

16. THE ACTS OF THE APOSTLES: OVERVIEW

Luke's Acts of the Apostles (perhaps more aptly identified as the Acts of the Holy Spirit!) is the second volume of his gospel. The date, situation, community composition, etc. are the same as that given in your Overview of Luke's gospel. Luke's purpose is to continue the major themes begun in the first volume. He presents his understanding of salvation history by showing how the ministry and mission of the Church, as exemplified in the two great figures of Peter and Paul, continue the mission and ministry begun by Jesus in Luke's gospel.

AN OUTLINE OF THE BOOK OF THE ACTS OF THE APOSTLES

I. INTRODUCTION TO THE ERA OF THE CHURCH (1:1-26)

(A) Witnesses' Commission and Jesus' Ascension (1:1-14)
    (1) Introduction (1-8)
    (2) The Ascension (1:9-14)
(B) The Restoration of the Twelve Apostles (1:15-26)

II. THE MISSION IN JERUSALEM (2:1–5:42)

(A) The Appeal to Israel (2:1–3:26)
    (1) The Pentecost Event (2:1-13)
    (2) The Pentecost Sermon (2:14-17)
    (3) First Major Summary (2:42-47)
    (4) The Healing in the Temple (3:1-11)
    (5) Peter's Temple Sermon (3:12-26)
(B) The Life and Trials of the Apostolic Church (4:1–5:42)
    (1) Peter and John Before the Sanhedrin (4:1-22)
    (2) The Apostles' Prayer (4:23-31)
    (3) Second Major Summary (4:32-35)
    (4) Singular Cases (4:36-5:11)
    (5) Third Major Summary (5:12-16)
    (6) The Second Persecution (5:17-42)

III. THE MISSION'S OUTWARD PATH FROM JERUSALEM (6:1–15:35)

(A) The Hellenists and Their Message (6:1–8:40)
    (1) The Commission of Seven Deacons (6:1-7)
    (2) The Testimony of Stephen (6:8-8:3)
        (a) Mission and Trial (6:8-7:1)
        (b) Stephen's Speech (7:2-53)
        (c) Stephen's Martyrdom (7:54-8:3)
    (3) Philip and the Advance of the Word (8:4-40)
        (a) Gospel's Triumph in Samaria (8:4-25)
        (b) Philip and the Ethiopian Eunuch (8:26-40)
(B) Paul's Persecution and Conversion (9:1-31)
    (1) The Conversion of Saul (9:1-19)
    (2) Saul in Damascus (9:19-25)
    (3) Saul in Jerusalem (9:26-31)
(C) Peter as Missionary (9:32–11:18)
    (1) Miracles in Lydda and Joppa (9:32-43)
    (2) The Conversion of Cornelius and His Household (10:1–11:18)
        (a) Cornelius' Vision (10:1-8)
        (b) Peter's Vision (10:9-16)
        (c) The Messengers' Reception (10:17-23)
        (d) Proceedings in Cornelius' House (10:23-48)
        (e) Peter's Accounting in Jerusalem (11:1-18)
(D) Between Jerusalem and Antioch (11:19–12:25)
    (1) The First Church of the Gentile Mission (11:19-30)
    (2) Herod's Persecution and Peter's Escape (12:1-25)
(E) The First Missionary Journey of Paul (13:1–14:28)
    (1) Prelude to the Journey (13:1-3)
    (2) Paul in Cyprus (13:4-12)
    (3) Mission and Rejection in Pisidian Antioch (13:13-52)
        (a) Paul's Sermon (13:13-43)
        (b) Turning to Gentiles (13:44-52)
    (4) Mixed Receptions in Central Asia Minor (14:1-20)
        (a) Iconium (14:1-7)
        (b) Lystra and Derbe (14:8-20)
    (5) Return to Antioch (14:21-28)
(F) The Jerusalem Conference (15:1-35)
    (1) Prehistory (15:1-5)
    (2) Peter's Appeal to Precedent (15:6-12)
    (3) James's Confirmation and Amendments (15:13-21)
    (4) Resolving the Issues (15:22-29)
    (5) Aftermath (15:30-35)

IV. PAUL'S PATH TO ROME (15:36–20:38)

(A) The Major Missions of Paul (15:36–20:38)
    (1) Mission Journeys Resumed (15:36-41)
    (2) The Road to Europe (16:1-10)
        (a) Timothy's Circumcision (16:1-5)
        (b) Paul's Vision (16:6-10)
    (3) The Mission in Greece (16:11–18:17)
        (a) Philippi (16:11-40)
        (b) Thessalonica (17:1-9)
        (c) Beroea (17:10-15)
        (d) Athens (17:16-34)
        (e) Corinth (18:1-17)
    (4) Return to Antioch and Journeys Resumed (18:18-23)
    (5) The Mission in Ephesus (18:24-19:40)
        (a) Apollos' Ministry (18:24-28)
        (b) The Baptist's Disciples (19:1-7)
        (c) Paul's Words and Wonders (19:8-20)
        (d) The Silversmiths' Riot and Paul's Departure (19:21-40)
    (6) Final Travels Between Asia and Greece (20:1-16)
        (a) To Greece and Troas (20:1-6)
        (b) Eutychus Resurrected (20:1-7)
        (c) Troas to Miletus (20:13-16)
    (7) Paul's Farewell Speech (20:17-38)
(B) Paul as Prisoner and Defendant in Palestine (21:1–26:32)
    (1) Return to Caesarea (21:1-4)
    (2) Paul's Imprisonment and Defense in Jerusalem (21:15–23:11)
        (a) Paul's Reception (21:15-26)
        (b) Riot and Imprisonment (21:27-36)
        (c) Paul's Defense and Appeal to Roman Law (21:37-22:29)
        (d) Paul Before the Sanhedrin (22:30–23:11)
(C) Paul Before Governor and King at Caesarea (23:12–26:32)
    (1) Transfer to Caesarea (23:12-35)
    (2) The Governor's Hearing (24:1-23)
    (3) Paul's Confinement (24:24-27)
    (4) Appeal to Caesar (25:1-12)
    (5) Referral to King Agrippa (25:13-22)
    (6) Paul Before King Agrippa (25:23–26:32)
(D) Paul's Last Journey and Ministry in Rome (27:1–28:31)
    (1) The Journey to Rome (27:1–28:16)
        (a) Sea Voyage, Shipwreck, and Deliverance (27:1-44)
        (b) Paul on Malta (28:1-10)
        (c) Arrival in Rome (28:11-16)
    (2) Paul in Rome (28:17-31)

To demonstrate the growth and development of the early Church, Luke uses:

Geographical Expansion as the disciples witness to the Word beginning in Jerusalem, then to Judea, Samaria, Antioch, Asia Minor, Greece, and finally Rome (which would represent symbolically the ends of the earth 1:8).

Speeches/Discourses which can be
Missionary (meant to convert)
Apologetic (in one's defense at a court trial)
Explanatory (to provide the real meaning of an event)

Repetitions of important events, the use of a pattern for the spread of the Word: preaching to Jews first, but rejection then turning to Gentiles, getting acceptance but further hostility and persecution occur so missionaries move on to the next town.

Summary Statements to remind the reader of the Church's growth, development, and characteristic lifestyle.

Parallelism between the patterns of the GOSPEL and ACTS, and between Jesus and the apostles and deacons in Acts (e.g. Peter, Paul, Stephen, Philip) to demonstrate how the ministry and mission of the Church are founded upon and continue that of Jesus. There is also a parallelism between Peter (Jewish Church) and Paul (Gentile Church).

THEMES IN ACTS:

(Many of the themes of Luke's gospel continue in Acts. Consult your Overview of Luke's Gospel.)

Fulfillment of God's Plan for Salvation:
Salvation history continues through the ministry and mission of the community of disciples, i.e. the Church.

The Triumph of Christianity Despite All Obstacles:
Since the existence and growth of the Christian community of disciples are part of God's plan for our salvation, neither natural nor supernatural obstacles can hinder its fulfillment.

Jesus Acting through the Spirit-filled Disciples:
After the gift of the Holy Spirit at Pentecost, the disciples continue the preaching and healing work that Jesus began. They also suffer persecution as Jesus did.

New Leadership for God's People:
The apostles replace the Jewish Sanhedrin as the authoritative teachers and leaders of God's people.

Healing and Restoration:
Healing is a sign of restoration and salvation — as it is in the gospel. Luke carefully distinguishes healing from magic, e.g. in chapters 8 and 19.

Continuity Amidst Change:
The major changes in the constitution of the Christian community are reflected in Acts. The transition from a predominantly Jewish-Christian community to that of Gentile-Christians has occurred. Luke depicts this transition as part of God's plan for them.

God's Guidance of the Christian "Way":
God's guidance of the Christian community is evident from the proliferation of references to God's Holy Spirit. The Spirit or breath of God shows God actively working for our salvation. This occurs in a wide variety of ways, e.g. appearances, visions, dreams, angels, prophecies, etc. Human decisions and actions are orchestrated by God to achieve the divinely-willed results.

Apologetic [Defense] for Christianity and for Paul:
Luke stresses that Christians are not a threat to the order of the Roman law. Further, the Jewish Christians, including Paul, remain faithful to the demands of the Jewish Law. The decision to admit Gentiles without circumcision and submission to Jewish Law came from God since it was arrived at through the power of the Holy Spirit.

17. PAUL: THE MAN AND HIS LETTERS

By Macrina Scott, O.S.F.

One of the beautiful things about the times in which we live is that we are becoming aware of the special gifts brought to the human community by minority groups among us: ethnic minorities, the increasing minority that live singly rather than with husband or wife, the minority who suffer physical handicaps, and many others. At the same time we are becoming aware of the special burdens that have been placed on minorities through the ages, and we admire their struggles today to achieve full recognition of their human rights and dignity. I have never heard of any official patron for minorities, and I would like to nominate St. Paul the Apostle for that position.

We should know Paul well, since we hear a passage from one of his letters in church most Sundays. The trouble is that if we do not know the man Paul and the struggles in which he was involved, the bits we hear may mean no more than overheard scraps of conversation between strangers. Let's take a closer look at this man who composed some of history's most famous letters. Understanding St. Paul can lead us to a better understanding of the early Church and of his important contribution to the New Testament.

Paul was bilingual and bicultural. He was born into both the majority culture of his time, the Hellenistic, and a minority culture, the Jewish. All his life he tried to deal with this double heritage and the conflicts inherent in it. He boasted both of being a Roman citizen, born in Tarsus, an important Hellenistic city, and of being a Jew and a member of the most strict religious group within Judaism, the Pharisees.

Saul the Jew

As a Jew, Paul spoke a language the New Testament calls Hebrew, though scholars today call it Aramaic to distinguish it from the more ancient form of the language in which the Hebrew Scriptures were written.

From the day of his birth, every detail of Paul's life was governed by the Jewish Law. When he was eight days old he was circumcised and given the name of Saul, the first king of Israel and most famous member of the new baby's tribe, the tribe of Benjamin. From childhood, Saul must have been taught to honor the ancestors of his people; he spoke of them in the letters he wrote long after (Romans 4:1-25; Galatians 4:21–31).

He went regularly to the synagogue with other Jewish boys of his age to learn to read and write Hebrew and, especially, to begin to memorize the 613 rules by which the daily life of the faithful Jew was regulated. These rules, basically the same as those observed by orthodox Jews today, seem to the outsider very burdensome. Kosher food laws are so complicated as to make it practically impossible for the orthodox Jew to eat anything not prepared in a special kitchen carefully supervised by someone who knows all the relevant laws.

Sabbath day regulations rigidly forbid most of the ordinary activities of life every Saturday. Sexual morality strictly guards family life, not only forbidding any violation of marital faithfulness, but even telling a married couple on which days they may or may not have intercourse! There are many prescribed prayers to be said, both privately and in the family. The young Saul was raised to think of all these not as oppressive rules but as a precious gift from God, the Law which enabled God's Chosen People to live in a way worthy of their high calling in every detail of their lives. The young Saul responded with enthusiasm.

Long after, he would remember: "I was circumcised on the eighth day, being of the stock of

Israel and the tribe of Benjamin, a Hebrew of Hebrew origins; in legal observance I was a Pharisee, and so zealous I persecuted the Church. I was above reproach when it came to justice based on the Law" (Philippians 3:5–6). And "I made progress in Jewish observance far beyond most of my contemporaries, in my excess of zeal to live out all the traditions of my ancestors" (Galatians 1:14).

At some point, the young Saul was brought (or sent) by his family to the center of the Jewish world, Jerusalem. There he mingled with ardent Jews from all over the world, as young American seminarians today mingle in Rome with others from around the world. There he participated in the splendid Temple liturgy, as pilgrims today participate in the great celebrations at St. Peter's which do so much to enkindle their enthusiasm for their faith and their Church.

Even more important, he received his graduate education in the intricacies of Jewish Law at the feet of one of the great teachers of the time, Gamaliel. Long after, when he was arrested at the instigation of a Jewish mob in Jerusalem, he would recall his early experience in that city with pride. When Roman soldiers had rescued him from a Jewish mob, he turned to address his own people: "My brothers and fathers, listen to what I have to say to you in my defense." When they heard him addressing them in Hebrew, they grew quieter still. He went on: "I am a Jew, born in Tarsus in Cilicia, but I was brought up in this city. Here I sat at the feet of Gamaliel and was educated strictly in the Law of our fathers. I was a staunch defender of God, just as all of you are today" (Acts 22:1-3).

As a Jew, Saul belonged to a small minority group within the Roman Empire. It was a close-knit group, held together both by religious traditions and by strong family, social and economic bonds. A Jewish traveler could go to any city of the Roman Empire, sure of finding there a Jewish section where he would find hospitality. The Roman Empire had no Social Security system, but a Jew who fell on hard times could depend on help from

the Jewish community. Then, as now, Jews sometimes suffered from the hostility of other citizens who were suspicious of anyone different from themselves. Danger coming from such hostility tightened the bonds within the Jewish community. Like any persecuted minority, they worked together to find ways of coping with oppression and with the anger which naturally arises from it. One of those ways was a great emphasis on their religious and moral superiority to the pagan majority that surrounded them. It was a very real superiority (Galatians 2:15).

Paul the Hellenist

This little Jewish community in Tarsus was an island surrounded by a pagan culture very foreign to it. Scholars label this majority culture the Hellenistic. It was the result of Alexander the Great's conquest of the East. He had brought Greek culture, along with the Greek language, everywhere. But the subjugated peoples combined what he brought with local elements. When the Roman Empire overcame the Greek, the Romans were glad to make use of the cosmopolitan culture that had developed, and of the form of the Greek language that had developed with it, *Koine* Greek.

Saul was born into this larger world as well as into his Jewish world. Like many Jewish children, he was given a second name, similar in sound to his Jewish name, but more familiar to non-Jews, and so easier to use in any dealings he had to have with them. This name is Paul. He learned the *Koine* Greek in which he would later preach and write his letters.

Paul wrote his letters in a style that showed he had some education in the majority culture in addition to his Hebrew studies. His family had the special privilege of being Roman citizens, and Paul later made use of the legal protection that privilege gave him (Acts 16:35-39; 25:10-12).

But at the same time that Paul carried in his heart the minority attitudes of his religious upbringing, he was taught to avoid contamination from the majority culture as much as possible. He was forbidden to eat its food or attend the violent games that provided its popular entertainment. He learned to despise its sexual licentiousness, and its casual worship of a multitude of gods, many of them as immoral as their worshipers. He learned, as part of his daily prayer, to thank God he had not been created a slave, a woman or a Gentile.

However, he also learned that a minority cannot ignore a majority on which it depends for survival. Within the Jewish community itself there were very different attitudes toward the majority culture. In Jerusalem, he met some Jews who hated the Hellenistic culture, refused to learn its language and avoided contact with pagans as much as they could. In Tarsus, it would have been hard to survive with such an attitude. Practically all Jews there spoke Greek. Some no longer spoke Hebrew, so it was necessary to translate the Hebrew Scriptures into Greek for their use.

Synagogues in Tarsus had to deal with the same problems as ethnic parishes in America, where many young people do not know the language of their grandparents. Around Paul's time, a few Jewish scholars like Philo and Josephus entered into the mainstream sufficiently to be able to write books in Greek, explaining Judaism in a way the Hellenistic reader could respect. But some members of the Jewish community disapproved of such compromise.

Compromise did not occur only on one side. Like other majorities, the Hellenists felt a mixture of contempt and fear and curiosity toward residents of the Jewish ghetto. While most kept their distance, a few, perhaps disillusioned with their own culture, were drawn toward the Jews. They were especially impressed by the Jewish worship of one God. They attended synagogue services and became known as "God-fearers." Perhaps the young Saul met some of them at his synagogue in Tarsus. Certainly, these borderline Hellenists would provide the most fertile field for his later missionary work.

Two Worlds in Conflict

So Paul grew up in two worlds, worlds which were in sharp conflict, but could not be kept completely separate. He was always to live with the tension of this double heritage. He valued both the sacred heritage of Judaism and the broader Hellenistic culture that made him a citizen of the world. He loved his own Jewish people, but he could not ignore those pagans with whom his parents forbade him to play. He never tells us what it was like to grow up as a Jewish boy in the Hellenistic city of Tarsus, or what it was like to move later from Tarsus to Jerusalem. But those who have grown up within minority groups in the United States today probably have a good idea of the complications of his life.

As an adult Paul continued to feel the impact of his double heritage. It was as a zealous Jew that he raged against the first Christians, whom he saw as heretics threatening the unity of the Jewish people. On that fateful journey to Damascus, when he was blinded by the brilliant light and fell to the ground, he heard the voice of Jesus speaking to him in Hebrew, but Jesus quoted a Greek proverb to him, "It is hard for you to kick against the goad." The Lord, who speaks so individually to each of us, knew that he spoke to a bicultural man, capable of responding to the speech of both Jews and Greeks. This was the man he had chosen to bring to the Hellenistic world the revelation made to the Jews (Acts 26:4-18).

Paul the Christian

After his conversion, Paul spent some time in Arabia and preached the gospel in Damascus, but something kept calling him back to Jerusalem, the center of his Jewish world. With some hesitation he was accepted by the Jewish Christian community in Jerusalem, but soon his zeal became more than they could endure. Perhaps some feared that his vigorous and controversial views would stir up hostility against the infant Church among the

Self-Portrait of St. Paul

I was circumcised when I was a week old. I am an Israelite by birth, of the tribe of Benjamin, a pure-blooded Hebrew. As far as keeping the Jewish Law is concerned, I was a Pharisee, and I was so zealous that I persecuted the Church. As far as a person can be righteous by obeying the commands of the Law, I was without fault. But all those things that I might count as profit I now reckon as loss for Christ's sake. Not only those things; I reckon everything as complete loss for the sake of what is so much more valuable, the knowledge of Christ Jesus my Lord. For his sake I have thrown everything away; I consider it all as mere garbage, so that I may gain Christ and be completely united with him. I no longer have a righteousness of my own, the kind that is gained by obeying the Law. I now have the righteousness that is given through faith in Christ, the righteousness that comes from God and is based on faith. All I want is to know Christ and to experience the power of his resurrection, to share in his sufferings and become like him in his death in the hope that I myself will be raised from death to life.

I do not claim that I have already succeeded or have already become perfect. I keep striving to win the prize for which Christ Jesus has already won me to himself. Of course, my brothers, I really do not think that I have already won it; the one thing I do, however, is to forget what is behind me and do my best to reach what is ahead. So I run straight toward the goal in order to win the prize, which is God's call through Christ Jesus to the life above.

Philippians 3:5-14

Christians' friends and relatives who had not yet accepted Jesus. Certainly his own life was in danger. His fellow Christians slipped him away to the nearest seaport and put him on the first ship to Hellenistic Tarsus. They may have sensed that the Jewish world of Jerusalem was too small for him (Acts 9:26-30).

After that, the main work of Paul was in bringing the Hellenists into the Church. But he never ceased thinking of himself as a Jew. Wherever his missionary journeys took him, on the first Sabbath after his arrival he attended the local synagogue, as any traveling Jew would do. There he preached Christ until the Jewish authorities put him out, forcing him to preach among the Gentiles.

He wrote in strong terms about the pain he felt at being rejected by his own people. "What I want to say is this: My sorrow is so great, and my mental anguish so endless, I would willingly be condemned and be cut off from Christ if it could help my brothers of Israel, my own flesh and blood. They were adopted as sons, they were given the glory and the covenants; the Law and the ritual were drawn up for them, and the promises were made to them. They are descended from the patriarchs and from their flesh and blood came Christ who is above all, God forever blessed!" (Romans 9:2-5).

Again and again he would return to Jerusalem, reporting on his missionary work, consulting with the Jewish Christian leaders, bringing financial contributions from the Hellenistic converts as an offering of peace. But it was not easy for the Jews, long proud of their religious and moral superiority, to accept former pagans as part of their community. They were suspicious of a Jew who was as much involved with outsiders as Paul was.

Paul, the bicultural man, never escaped the tension between his two worlds. Though the members of his minority group persecuted him for his involvement with the majority, he continued to identify with the Jewish community. He lamented that he had been beaten five times by synagogue officials (a thing they could not have done had he not considered himself under their jurisdiction), and that he was often "in danger from my own people" (2 Corinthians 11: 24-26). It is when he had gone to the Temple in Jerusalem to pray that he was finally attacked by a Jewish mob and eventually sent to Rome for trial.

However, Paul also suffered because his Hellenistic converts, brought up to despise Jews, sometimes continued to feel superior. He describes the relationship between Jew and Hellenist within the Christian community with the image of an olive tree. "No doubt some of the branches have been cut off, and, like shoots of wild olive, you have been grafted among the rest to share with them the rich sap provided by the olive tree itself, but still, even if you think yourself superior to the other branches, remember that you do not support the root; it is the root that supports you. You will say, 'Those branches were cut off on purpose to let me be grafted in.' True, they were cut off, but through their unbelief; if you still hold firm, it is only thanks to your faith. Rather than making you proud, that should make you afraid" (Romans 11:17-20).

Paul, the Jewish missionary to the Gentile world, suffered from both the anti-Hellenism of the Jews and the anti-Semitism of the Hellenists. For Saul-Paul, his bilingual, bicultural background was the source both of the deepest tensions in his life and his greatest effectiveness as a Christian missionary.

Paul the Single Person

Paul also belonged to another minority: that minority of adults who live alone, rather than as part of a couple. This group includes adults who have never married and those who are widowed or divorced. Paul does not tell us to which of the three he belonged. Since Jewish Law required young men to marry, it is unlikely that so fervent a law-abiding Jew as he failed to marry in his youth.

Since divorce was permitted by Jewish Law, he may have divorced his wife, or she may have died. The thing that is important for singles today is to know that he shared with them the particular possibilities and burdens that are common to the never-married, the widowed and the divorced.

He makes it clear that he valued his single life because it left him a greater freedom for serving the Lord: "I would like to see you free from all worry. An unmarried man can devote himself to the Lord's affairs, all he need worry about is pleasing the Lord; but a married man has to bother about the world's affairs and devote himself to pleasing his wife: he is torn two ways" (1 Corinthians 7:32-33).

The warm way he speaks of many friends in various cities shows that he also made use of the freedom single life can give to cultivate a wide variety of friends (Romans 16:1-16; 1 Corinthians 16:10-20; Philippians 2:19-30; Colossians 4:7-14).

At the same time, his very eagerness to be reunited with absent friends suggests that he also knew the loneliness that goes with the single life (2 Corinthians 7:5-7).

Paul the Handicapped

Paul also belonged to a third minority: that of the physically handicapped. Some scholars think that he was an epileptic, but we cannot be sure about that. We only know that Paul writes to the Corinthians about some chronic ailment which he has suffered for fourteen years, and that he writes to the Galatians about an ailment of a disgusting kind he suffered while with them (2 Corinthians 12:7-10; Galatians 4:12-14). We are not even sure both passages refer to the same problem.

But what makes Paul a model for all handicapped persons — and who is not handicapped in some way? — is that he finds a spiritual value in the very fact of his weakness: "About this thing, I have pleaded with the Lord three times for it to leave me, but he has said, 'My grace is enough for you; my power is at its best in weakness.' So I shall be very happy to make my weaknesses my special boast so that the power of Christ may stay over me, and that is why I am quite content with weaknesses.... For it is when I am weak that I am strong" (2 Corinthians 12:9-10).

Paul never escaped the tensions that came from his bilingual, bicultural background, the loneliness that goes with the single life or the weakness of a physical handicap. Yet God chose him to be a pioneer in bringing the Good News of Jesus to the whole world. He is an example of the very special gifts that members of minority groups often bring to the human community.

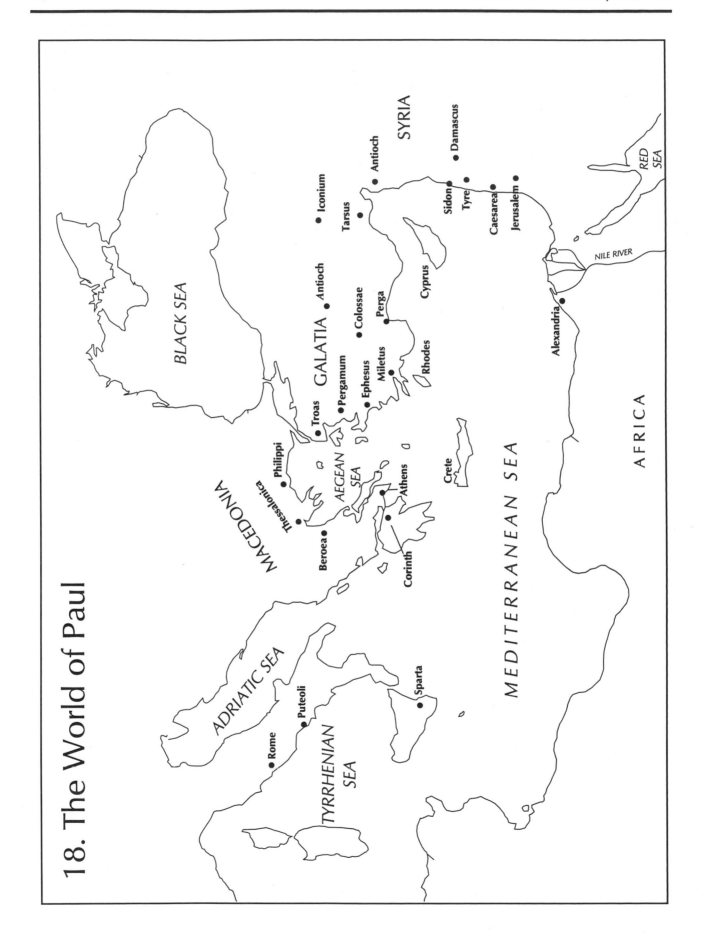

18. The World of Paul

19. A CHRONOLOGY OF PAUL'S LIFE

For many of the dates only a general approximation can be made. For a fuller discussion of Paul's chronology, see Joseph Fitzmyer, S.J., "Paul" in *The New Jerome Biblical Commentary,* pp. 1329-1337. This chronology follows that of Fitzmeyer.

DATES (A.D.)	EVENTS IN PAUL'S LIFE	SCRIPTURE REFERENCES	PAUL'S LETTERS	HISTORICAL EVENTS
c. 1-10 (?)	birth of Paul	Acts 7:58, Phlm 1:9		
c. 20-30 (?)	Jerusalem studies	Acts 22:3, 26:4		Death of Caesar
36	stoning of Stephen; Paul's conversion	Acts 7:58, 9:1-19, 22:4-20, Gal 1:13-16		Augustus, 14 A.D. Pilate procurator from 26 to 36
37-40	in Damascus, Arabia, again in Damascus	Acts 9:20-22, 23-25 Gal 1:17		Death of Jesus, 30
40	First journey to Jerusalem (15 days)	Acts 9:26-28 Gal 1:18-20		Death of Tiberius, 37 Death of Caligula, 41
40-44	in Tarsus	Acts 9:29-30 Gal 1:21-24		Death of Agrippa I, 44 Claudius expels Jews
44-46	in Antioch	Acts 11:25-26		from Rome, 49 (Acts 18:2)
46-49	FIRST MISSIONARY JOURNEY (Cyprus and Asia Minor)	Acts 13-14 2 Tim 3:11		
49	Famine, second Jerusalem journey to bring contributions	Acts 11:27-30, 12:25		
49	Apostolic meeting in Jerusalem	Acts 15:1-35 Gal 2:1-10		
49	Dispute with Cephas in Antioch	Gal 2:11-14		
49	SECOND MISSIONARY JOURNEY begins	Acts 15:36-18:22 Gal 4:13-15		
50	Philippi, Thessalonica, Athens	Acts 16:11-40, 17:1-9, 16-34		
50-52	Corinth	18:1-17	1 Thessalonians 2 Thessalonians (?)	Gallio proconsul in Achaia, 52-53
52-54	Antioch	Acts 18:22		
54	THIRD MISSIONARY JOURNEY begins	Acts 18:23 - 21:17		
	Galatia-Phrygia	Acts 18:23		Death of Claudius, 54
54-57	Ephesus	Acts 19	Philippians 1 Corinthians 2 Corinthians	
57	Departure from Ephesus, in Macedonia	Acts 20:1-6		
57-58	Corinth (winter)	Acts 20:3	Galatians Romans	
58	To Macedonia, Philippi, Jerusalem, arrest	Acts 20:3–23:25		
58-60	imprisoned in Caesarea	Acts 24-26		
60-61	Sea voyage to Rome wreck at Malta arrival in Rome	Acts 27–28:16		Porcius Festus procurator, 60-62
61-63	in prison	Acts 28:17-31	Philemon Colossians (?)	
63-65	?? Another journey: Ephesus, Macedonia, Nicopolis, Crete, back to Rome	1 Tim 1:3 Tit 1:5, 3:12	Ephesians (??) 1 Timothy (??) Titus (??)	Burning of Rome, 64
66-67	?? again in prison in Rome	2 Tim 1:15-18 4:9-21	2 Timothy (??)	Roman persecution of Christians Jewish revolt in Judea, 66-73
67	Martyrdom under Nero			
				Death of Nero, 68 Jerusalem Temple destroyed, 70

20. HOW TO GET TO THE HEART OF A PAULINE LETTER

Since most letters represent one side of a dialogue carried on in writing over a distance rather than face to face, the more one knows about the life situation of the parties to the dialogue, the more one can reasonably expect to understand the dialogue. The best preparation for understanding Paul's letters, therefore, is a familiarity with his life and with the life situation of the early Christians in Asia Minor, Greece, and Rome to whom Paul wrote.

The next best preparation is to read the letters as letters, keeping in mind that in basic form and psychology Paul's letters do not differ from letters written today. Thus his practice of hinting at or anticipating in the thanksgiving the central concern that has prompted him to write the letter is not unlike the common practice today of carefully phrasing the opening of a letter in order to set the stage for the more important subject matter of the body of the letter.

Paul's practice of using a theoretical or dogmatic exposition as a preparation for the solution of a practical problem should help the reader to discover a link between the doctrinal instruction and the ethical exhortation. The reader should attend carefully to the problem Paul faces and then analyze his solution of the problem in relation to the doctrinal points he makes in leading up to his solution.

The reader should remember that problems dealt with in one letter lead in later letters to more nuanced solutions and to a consequent deeper penetration of the earlier theological teaching. Paul's solution to the problem of the parousia and the resurrection in 1 Thessalonians, for example, is followed a few years later by the deeper penetration of the resurrection in 1 Corinthians and Romans. Also, it is possible to discern a development of Paul's theology of faith and justification from his initial exposition of the problem in Gala-tians 2:15-3:29 to his final, masterful exposition of the same problem in Romans 1-11.

Finally, the reader should realize that Paul's letters have both the advantages and the disadvantages inherent in communication by letter. They have all the spontaneity, sincerity, warmth, and interest of personal communication, but at the same time they have the brevity, tentativeness, and incompleteness so typical of letters. Unlike literary works, letters cannot be revised or re-edited; all the writer can do is write another letter. It is for this reason that we have a second letter to the Corinthians and a more nuanced and more profound version of Galatians' argumentation on faith and justification in Paul's later letter to the Romans.

from Peter F. Ellis,
Seven Pauline Letters,
(Collegeville: The Liturgical Press, 1982), p. 12.

21. SIX LETTERS FROM ST. PAUL:

HELPING REAL PEOPLE SOLVE REAL PROBLEMS

By Steve Mueller

If you have ever wrestled with St. Paul's letters, you would probably be surprised at his claim that "I never write anything you cannot read and understand" (2 Cor 1:13). We would probably agree more with the author of the second letter of Peter who expresses the real truth — "in them [Paul's letters] there are some things hard to understand" (2 Pt 3:16). This doesn't mean we should give up on Paul. But his letters will always be challenging.

Things have improved, however, since the Second Vatican Council. Prior to the Council, most of us had limited acquaintance with St. Paul's letters. We heard snippets of his letters at Mass, and only the bravest homilist ever dared to preach on these passages. Theologians quoted well-chosen lines from Paul as "proof texts" for the doctrines they debated. Like a ventriloquist's dummy, Paul was made to say only what we wanted him to say. The bottom line was that Paul's message for us often got lost. Why? We tried so hard to lift out his abstract theological ideas that we paid too little attention to the specific situations and problems that Paul and his communities were facing.

Vatican II's *Dogmatic Constitution on Divine Revelation* corrects this misguided approach to Paul. It insists that to get the meaning Paul intended, we must put his letters into their proper contexts. This means we must first read each letter as a whole to discover how the parts fit together. Then we must read all his letters to learn how Paul's thinking changed during the course of his ministry. Finally, we must read the letters against the background of the world Paul lived in. If we read this way, Paul can once again speak for himself.

When we let this happen, we also find a new way to look at Paul's theology. By bringing Paul's world to life, we rediscover that his theology is not just a haphazard collection of ideas. It was meant to help real people solve real problems. The great abstract themes of our theology — Christ, church, sin, salvation, sacraments, etc. — are not separated out by Paul but are part of his practical concern to help his communities discover a new Christian way of life.

Paul's Theology for the New "Way"

Before Christianity was called Christianity, it was called "The Way." It was both a new way to relate to God and a new way of life. After Paul was converted from a persecutor of "The Way" to a follower, he spent his life proclaiming this new Way and explaining its demands to his converts.

Paul's theology always begins with the community's situation and the everyday problems that they face. Paul's method for doing theology is to take a hard look at the community's problems and illuminate them with the light of God's revelation of salvation through Jesus Christ. Those everyday problems then become *theo-logical*, i.e. understood only in relation to God's plan for setting us into the right relation with God. Finally, Paul's theological solution leads to practical changes in behavior. He provides many guidelines for leading a Christian life in a culture which had not yet been confronted by Christian beliefs or behavior.

Here we will consider only the letters associated with St. Paul which scripture scholars agree to be Paul's own. (Because of its brevity and since it is addressed to an individual rather than a community, we are omitting the letter to Philemon even though it is considered a genuine writing of Paul.) Although the other letters attributed to Paul might contribute further clues to Paul's theology, these genuine letters are our surest source for Paul's own thinking about how to understand our new relation to God and how to act in light of that understanding. We will also treat his letters in the probable order in which he wrote them. This approach differs significantly from their order in our Bible where they are grouped according to their length, with the longest letters first.

To the Church at Thessalonica (1):
Advice for Converts

When Paul's preaching journeys finally took him to Europe, he gathered one of his early communities in the thriving seaport city of Thessalonica. This was the capital of the northern area of Greece called Macedonia. As the hub of all the transportation flowing from Asia Minor into northern Greece, it attracted a diverse populace of Greeks and foreigners. Each group had its own style of religion. The new Christian "Way" attracted many followers.

In this earliest Christian document, dated about the year 50, Paul wrote about the meaning of Christian conversion. Paul had guided these Gentile converts (note the lack of quotes from the Hebrew Scriptures) to their new life in Christ. Then he had moved on. But like new converts today, their baptism did not solve all their problems. So they asked their former pastor Paul for help.

In a key passage early in this letter (1:9) Paul notes with praise how these new converts had "turned to God from idols, to serve the living and true God, and to await from heaven the Son he raised from the dead — Jesus who delivers us from the wrath to come." This three-part description — to turn, to serve, to await — summarizes the Christian conversion process and is indeed a good overview of the letter itself.

First, one must *turn* or change one's basic orientation from faith in many gods (polytheism) to faith in the one god (monotheism). It is interesting to note that Paul mentions all of the persons of the Trinity — and this barely 20 years after the death of Christ!

Second, one must *serve* God. This service involves suffering (2:14–3:8), a growth in holiness (3:9–4:8), and physical labor (4:9-12). In chapters 4 and 5, Paul gives many practical directives about sexual conduct, mutual charity, and community order.

Third, one must *await* with steadfast hope Jesus' glorious return. At this time Paul was still preaching the more immediate return of Jesus during his own lifetime (4:17). But as the years went by without this happening, both Paul and the Christian Church realized that this return would not be so soon.

But Paul's main concern is never on idle speculation about the future end but always on the present — on what kind of people we will be in view of the coming end. In Thessalonica, many were waiting in the wrong way. Some simply quit working. Others had misunderstood Paul's message about Jesus' return. So Paul reinstructs them first about their hope for their own resurrection because of the resurrection of Jesus and second about their conduct as they wait (4:13–5:11).

To the Church at Philippi:
Putting on the "Mind of Christ"

Philippi, named for King Philip of Macedon, the father of Alexander the Great, was probably the first city Paul evangelized in Europe. Located ten miles inland from the Aegean Sea, the Roman colony of Philippi was a center for mining, trade, and military defense. Many ex-soldiers retired there and provided a pro-Roman atmosphere to the town. A variety of religions and gods competed for people's attention and loyalty.

About the year 54, Paul writes to them from jail. We do not know exactly where he was, but Ephesus is a likely place. He thanks this beloved community for supporting him both after he left them to work in Thessalonica and now in prison.

In his letter, Paul wants to help them "learn to value the things that really matter" (1:10). Christian conversion demands a radical change in the way we evaluate our everyday lives. The community was sad because Paul was in prison. So Paul uses his own suffering and imprisonment as an example of this Christian revaluation. When viewed against the background of God's plan for our salvation, his suffering has a new meaning. It "has worked out to the furtherance of the gospel" (1:12). Despite the appearance of obstruction and failure, the gospel is being preached! And that is all that matters.

Paul describes this revaluing process as "putting on the mind of Christ" (2:5). Paul knew that if we could see and evaluate the world as Jesus did, we would behave like Jesus did. Like him, we would empty ourselves out of love for others. Then our world would really be transformed by our Christian behavior. By putting on the mind of Christ, the Philippian Christians will be able to conduct themselves "in a way worthy of the gospel" (1:27).

Paul again uses himself as an example of the demands of conversion. He had to put aside the Jewish way of life he loved (3:2-16). What he formerly valued highly, he now considers rubbish. What matters now is to know Christ and to be formed into the pattern of his death so that new life might emerge. Paul's own conversion struggles become a model for the community (3:17-21).

To the Church at Corinth (1):
The New Christian Sacredness

Corinth was a booming, wide-open city. Rebuilt by the Romans about a hundred years before Paul's time, it was the crossroads port of the whole Mediterranean. Like Los Angeles or New York, its population was socially, ethnically, and economically diverse. The fabulously rich, ordinary mer-

chants (like Paul, who was a leatherworker or tent-maker), wandering philosophers, sailors, slaves and prostitutes vied for the attention of the travelers who constantly passed through.

From this world of diverse and sharply divided classes, races, and religions, Paul shaped the community which gave him headaches as a pastor and challenged him even more to grow as a Christian. His first letter reveals his headaches, his second shows his personal growth.

Corinth offered its visitors and inhabitants a dizzying variety of pleasures — wisdom for the mind, sex for the body, and mystery religions for the spirit. Paul's first letter to this community sketches out his Christian alternatives — a new wisdom, a new sacredness for the body, and a new religious way of life.

In chapters 1-4, Paul sketches a "new wisdom" based on Christ and his cross. In its eagerness to adopt the new Christian way, the community had splintered into four different groups. Each claimed loyalty to its hero—Paul, Apollos, Peter, and Christ. Just as the existence of factions (the conservatives, liberals, and silent majority) causes confusion in our Church today, competing ways of following Christ had shaken their unity. But Paul reminds them that in Christ no factions can exist. Christians are not competing against one another, but building on the one foundation — Christ (3:11).

Paul also turns the usual types of wisdom upside down. Conventional wisdom taught that knowledge was the key to salvation, i.e., the right relation to God. Greek philosophers preached "Know yourself." Jewish scribes taught "Know the Law of Moses." Paul proclaimed only Christ crucified (2:2). He believed that the death and resurrection of Christ was the only way to God.

In chapters 5-10, Paul answers the communitiy's questions about how to act in the midst of their pagan environment. Can Christians commit incest, sue each other in the public courts, visit prostitutes, need to be married, or eat meat which had been slain at the city's religious temples before being sold at the public market? Paul's answers give them a new sense of the sacredness of their everyday lives amidst the prevailing practices of Corinth.

In each case, Paul's method is to help them to see their problem in relation to their relationship to Christ. Christians are "temples of God" (3:17) because God dwells in them. "Whoever is joined to the Lord becomes one spirit with Him" (6:17). Here Paul touches on the core truth of our sanctification from within by God's presence in us. Since God's indwelling power is making us holy, all of our outwardly ordinary behavior acquires a new motive — "whether you eat or drink — whatever you do — you should do all for the glory of God. Give no offense to Jew or Greek or to the church of God" (10:31-32).

In chapters 11–16, Paul responds to problems affecting the religious life of the community such as conduct at worship, celebrating the Eucharist, the regulation of spiritual gifts, the resurrection of the body, and the collection for the struggling church of Jerusalem. Paul's answers outline a new religious approach.

The key is Paul's appeal to the image of the community as the Body of Christ. In this classic image, Paul shows how unity can be achieved even in diversity. The great variety of the individual members and their gifts are joined through love into a greater unity for the sake of the body. Paul's image reminds us that the Christian "way" of community breaks down the natural and artificial boundaries which usually keep us so divided. Our Eucharistic celebration is the great enactment of this new Christian unity.

To the Church at Corinth (2):
The New Christian Discipleship

This is the most personal of all Paul's letters. Since Paul's departure from this community, new missionaries had passed through. They had criticized

Paul both for his personal weaknesses and for the doctrines he had preached. This set up a serious tension between the community and their former pastor.

Most of us are surprised by Paul's heated defense of his apostolic ministry. Is it just his ego? The intensity of his response reveals the theological character of his real motives. For Paul, the apostle and his message are the foundation of the community's faith. If the original message is false, then so will be the faith of the community. So Paul never allows anyone to question his apostolic claims or the gospel he preaches.

But strangely enough, where we would expect Paul to boast of his success and achievements to back up his claims for apostolic ministry, he boasts only of his sufferings! (See chapters 3–6, 11–12.) Paul knew from his own experience that the test of a Christian is how much that person has entered into the mystery of Christ's death and resurrection. Outward appearances mean nothing. The weakness of our "earthen vessels" is our real strength for it lets the power of God working through us be manifested brilliantly.

To the Churches in Galatia:
The New Christian Freedom

The Roman province of Galatia encompassed most of what is now central Turkey. Paul had traveled this area extensively on his second and third missionary journeys and no doubt founded many communities. His letter reads like a far-reaching circular letter which each community is to read and then pass on to others in the region.

By the mid-fifties, the tension between Jewish and Gentile converts to the new Christian way had turned bitter. Paul had received permission from the Jerusalem authorities to preach Christianity without obliging Gentile converts to adopt the obligations of the Jewish law (2:1-10, Acts 15). But after Paul had left Galatia, some Jewish–Christian missionaries approached his communities, teaching that Paul's version of Christianity was not genuine. They claimed that the Christian "way" had to pass through Judaism. This meant Paul's Gentile converts needed to adopt some practices of the Jewish Law if they wanted to be really Christian.

Paul's Galatian letter is a harsh and biting critique of these other missionaries and their misguided proposals. As he did with the Corinthians, Paul angrily defends his apostolic gift and the message he preached because they are the basis for the community's life.

But the real issue is what Paul teaches about salvation. Paul warns that there can be no other gospel because that would mean there was another way to God besides Christ. The Mosaic Law does not bring us into the right relation to God — only God can do that. And God chose to do this through Christ.

In this letter's argument about the role of the Law of Moses, Paul stresses the famous image of God's saving action as justification. Borrowing from what happens in a law court, Paul recognizes that although we are indeed guilty and deserving of punishment, instead God justifies us, i.e. God acquits us and frees us. God's justification frees us from obligation to the Jewish Law for a new life in Christ. Just as Abraham in the Jewish tradition was set in the right relation to God by his faith long before there was any Mosaic Law, so Christians are saved by their faith in Jesus Christ rather than by keeping the Jewish Law.

To the Church at Rome:
The 'Gospel' of Paul

After years of missionary activity in the eastern Mediterranean, Paul decided to go to Spain. But first, he wanted to return to Jerusalem to deliver the collection he had been taking up for the church there. Before leaving Corinth in the spring of 57, Paul wrote to the Roman community. Rome was the great metropolitan capital of the whole

Roman world. The Christian community there was at this time gaining prominence and soon Peter the Apostle would become its leader.

Although Paul did not found this community or know its members personally, he was eager to enlist their support for his missionary work. So he wrote to introduce himself and his "gospel" — the message of the Christian Way as he proclaimed it. It is a magnificent summary of Paul's theology and spirituality.

In chapters 1–4 Paul provides his overview of the experience of salvation. All humanity — both Gentile and Jew — through its sin had broken down its right relationship with God, and rightly deserved God's wrath. But God's saving action through Jesus Christ gives all humanity the possibility of a new relationship.

In chapters 5–8 Paul outlines the new Christian spirituality which flows from God's saving action. By accepting God's offer, "the love of God has been poured out into our hearts through the Holy Spirit that has been given to us" (5:5). The result is a life "in Christ" through which we are freed from the wrath of God (5), from the dominance of sin (6), from the obligations of the Mosaic Law (7), and from the tyranny of death (8). Christian living is the process of God working from within to transform us into a new creation.

In chapters 9–11, Paul reflects on the salvation of the Jews who have not become Christians. After a complicated argument, Paul concludes that in God's great plan of salvation even these will ultimately be joined to those who are saved. Such are the wonders of God's mercy!

In chapters 12–16, Paul gives practical advice about specific Christian behavior both within the community (12, 14) and in society (13), according to the model of Christ (15). We can still learn from his basic directive: "Do not conform yourself to this age but be transformed by the renewal of your mind, that you may discern what is the will of God, what is good and pleasing and perfect" (12:2).

Paul's Theology for Today's Churches

Paul's letters remind us that theology is meant to be practical. He shows us how the truths of the Christian message can be applied to our everyday problems. Doing theology links our faith and our life. As Vatican II has stressed, the "split between the faith many profess and their daily lives deserves to be counted among the more serious errors of our age" (*The Church in the Modern World*, #43).

St. Paul refused to foster this kind of "split" in dealing with the churches under his care. Paul asked us to be imitators of him (1 Cor 4:16), and we can do this by taking the rich faith he has shared with us and applying it creatively to the real problems and issues of our times.

22. THE LETTERS OF PAUL: OVERVIEWS

Paul

Paul, a Jew, was born in Tarsus. He was at home both with the Hellenistic or Greek culture of the Roman Empire and with the religious world of Judaism. As a Jew he was reared in the Jewish traditions. He professed to have been a Pharisee and in his zeal to have outstripped all others in his observance of the Mosaic Law. He was educated in the Greek manner, and was generally acquainted with Greek philosophy and rhetoric or public speaking skills. He was also educated in the Jewish manner, and was a skilled interpreter of the Jewish sacred writings.

Paul's whole life was changed by his personal encounter with the Risen Lord on the road to Damascus. This experience is the heart of his Christian life. As a result of this experience, Paul spent his lifetime in service to this "Lord Jesus." His service was primarily that of missionary evangelization and the building up of Christian communities.

Pauline Letters in General

Paul's letters were written prior to the four written gospels. He presupposes an awareness of the Christian message (e.g. sayings of Jesus, stories about Jesus, the Passion materials, accounts of the resurrection events) by his audience. On the basis of these beliefs, Paul is trying to convince and persuade the communities to adopt appropriate Christian behaviors. Normally Paul does not argue about doctrine; he simply states what is the belief of the Christian community. Paul's main aim is persuasion. He wishes to instruct about what Christians believe in order to deepen the readers' adherence to the Christian truth. But Paul also wishes to persuade the communities to change their lives and act in ways which express their beliefs in action.

In his letters, Paul is ultimately concerned with what happens to people after they experience the Risen Lord in faith. His concern is with Christian living as these new converts struggle to know Christ more fully and to live as Christians in their everyday lives. Their problems are the starting point for Paul's letters. His advice concerning particular problems is part of every letter. Paul always tries to get the communities to see their problems against the perspective of God's action for salvation through Jesus Christ.

From the general assumption that people's beliefs guide their behavior, Paul reinforces what they believe and argues for suitable behaviors. If you know who Christ is, you will know how to act as a Christian.

Structure of a Letter

The general pattern of a Pauline letter is similar to our pattern today.

1. SALUTATION:
   Mention of the sender, the recipient, and greeting.

2. THANKSGIVING:
   Recounting of the shared relationship; reasons for writing.

3. CENTRAL SECTION:
   The main "business" of the letter or problem-solving section.
   For Paul, this is usually done in the form of
   1. Doctrinal instruction, a reminder and clarification of Christian beliefs
   2. Exhortation to appropriate Christian behavior

4. CLOSING

1 THESSALONIANS

In NT times, Thessalonica, the capital of the Roman province of Macedonia, was a populous commercial center. During his second missionary journey, Paul formed a community here. But opposition from the Jews forced him to move on quickly (Acts 17:1-10).

Occasion:

(written 50-52 A.D. from Corinth)
The community has been suffering from harassment from its neighbors. Within the community, there is some confusion about the meaning of Paul's teaching on the *Parousia* or glorious return of Christ to earth. Paul's letter shows his joy and affection for this beloved community. He encourages them to faithfulness and constancy in their Christian life. He also tries to clear up some of the problems they experience with their Christian beliefs.

Principal Themes:

The first part of this letter reveals the earliest proclamation of the gospel that we have. Paul also reminds the people about his relations with them. We get an idea of how Paul worked and preached Christianity to these new Gentile converts (note the absence of any reference to the Old Testament in this letter!).

Paul must have proclaimed to them the importance of Jesus' return as a central part of God's plan for salvation. Since it was to happen soon, they wonder about the fate of those faithful Christians who have died before the actual time occurs.

Paul's Response:

Although Paul supposes that the second coming is NEAR, he reminds them that the EXACT time is uncertain and will remain so. Idle speculation trying to determine the exact time is useless. The community ought to turn its attention rather to how they are living NOW in preparation for the final end-time events. For the unprepared, the end will be a time to fear. For those prepared, it will be a time of consolation. One can be prepared only by unfailing vigilance and wakefulness (note the similarities of Paul's approach to that of the synoptic evangelists in their treatments of the end-time, e.g. Mark 13, Luke 21, Matthew 24–25). The challenge is to live out our Christianity and not just bide our time till the end. Since God cares for all, the dead are no worse off than the living when the final change of our world takes place.

2 THESSALONIANS

Occasion:

(50-52 if by Paul himself/
70's or later if by one of his followers)
Apparently the exhortations and teachings of 1 Thessalonians about the expectation of the *Parousia* or the practical demands of Christian behavior have not been heeded. In particular, the community has been disturbed by some who claim that the *Parousia* had already occurred. If, indeed, the letter was written by a follower of Paul, then perhaps the time after the fall of the temple in Jerusalem in 70 A.D. caused the Pauline communities to rethink their approach to the end time (as is clear from the synoptic evangelists struggling with this problem in each of their respective communities). In this case, the Pauline author wrote claiming the authority of Paul and modeled this letter on the approach laid out by Paul himself in 1 Thessalonians.

Paul's Response:

To counter their preoccupation about the exact date and the claim that the end had already occurred, he reminds the community of the traditions which he had taught them about the sequence of events which had to precede the end-time. Paul uses conventional images and ideas from contemporary Jewish Apocalyptic writings, e.g. the activity of "Satan," the coming of apostasy and the "man of lawlessness." But since these signs have not yet taken place, it is obviously wrong to claim that the end has already occurred.

PHILIPPIANS

Philippi — named for Philip of Macedon, the father of Alexander the Great — was probably the first city Paul evangelized in Europe on his second missionary journey. Located ten miles inland from the Aegean Sea, the Roman colony of Philippi was a center for mining, trade and military defense. Many ex-soldiers retired there and provided a pro-Roman atmosphere to the town.

Occasion:

(54-57 from prison in Ephesus,
or less likely 60-61 from Rome)
The community is troubled both by Paul's imprisonment and by struggles in their community which are leading to unrest and dissention. The community is also perplexed because some new missionaries have also appeared and their approach to Christianity (heavily Jewish, thus these are called "Judaizers") contrasts greatly with the approach they had learned from Paul.

Paul's Response

There seem to be three major divisions of this letter (which has led some scholars to suspect that the letter as we have it might be a composite rather than a single letter of Paul).

Paul thanks the community for their continued support. He reveals his personal situation in prison and teaches that his suffering is meaningful because it is part of God's plan for salvation. Paul recognizes the centrality of the cross in the life of the Christian disciple.

Paul attempts to deal with community problems by emphasizing the community's need for unity of mind and heart. They must put on the mind of Christ. Paul uses a familiar Christian hymn to express the core of Christ's attitude. Rather than

cling to his divine privileges, Christ emptied himself [*kenosis*] by becoming one of us and by obediently accepting his suffering on the cross. Consequently, God has exalted him and recognized him as Lord. For us too, who imitate Christ, the pattern will be through death to exaltation.

Paul warns the community against accepting the approach of the Judaizers. He reveals his own journey through Judaism to Christianity. But now he has re-evaluated everything in the light of Christ Jesus, the only way to salvation.

THE CORINTHIAN CORRESPONDENCE

Corinth was worldly, successful, sophisticated, possessing all that is best and worst in a major city. Paul first came to Corinth during his second missionary journey and spent around eighteen months there. Although it took much time and work, probably the largest Christian community in Greece was established there. Apollos, a convert from Alexandria, helped strengthen the community after Paul's initial efforts.

1 CORINTHIANS

Occasion:

(54-57 A.D. from Ephesus)
The special demands of the Christian lifestyle proved difficult for people living in the environment of Corinth. Abuses and misunderstandings arose regarding doctrine, morality, and discipline. In 1 CORINTHIANS, Paul addresses the community's problems and questions in each of these areas.

Principal Themes in 1 Corinthians:

1) DIVISIONS WITHIN THE CHRISTIAN COMMUNITY
   Factions had arisen based on affiliation with certain preachers and apostles. Growing out of such affiliations were special claims to wisdom.

Paul's Response:
What is lacking is the appreciation of belonging to one another as members of the Body of Christ. God's ministers can only build upon the one foundation, Jesus Christ, who should be the focus of the believer.

Christians are to live according to the wisdom of God (Christ crucified) and not according to human wisdom which is really foolishness in comparison.

2) MORAL ABUSES WITHIN THE CHRISTIAN COMMUNITY

SEXUAL IMMORALITY
[incest and fornication]
The community should take action against such occurrences and not sit idly by. Each person belongs to God as a member of Christ and a temple of the Holy Spirit, and should live accordingly.

LAWSUITS before pagan courts.
Christians should be able to settle their own disputes.

MARRIAGE AND CELIBACY
Paul's advice is conditioned by his culture and his expectation of the *Parousia*. Husbands and wives belong to each other, not to themselves. No divorce and remarriage. A "believing" spouse is not bound to an "unbelieving" spouse if the latter wishes to separate. (Yet, perhaps the "believing" spouse can be a source of salvation for the "unbeliever.") While both lifestyles are good, marriage provides natural distractions which may keep one from concentrating on the Lord's coming as one should. But, better to marry than to "burn." In order to avoid great distraction, it is better to remain in one's current state of life.

MEAT OFFERED TO IDOLS
Whatever is done should be done for the glory of God. Give no scandal.

3) ABUSES WITHIN THE CELEBRATION OF EUCHARIST

PAUL'S RESPONSE TO WOMEN'S DRESS:
Conditioned by his culture as well as OT attitudes. Men should "look like" men and women should "look like" women.

PAUL'S RESPONSE TO DIVISIONS WITHIN THE CELEBRATING COMMUNITY:
The Eucharist should be a common meal where there is personal concern and involvement with each other for it to have true meaning. There should be no overeating, no overdrinking, no factions. This meal is to be celebrated in remembrance of the Lord, proclaiming his death until he comes.

4) MISUNDERSTANDINGS REGARDING SPIRITUAL GIFTS

Paul's Response:
All spiritual gifts are given at the discretion of the Holy Spirit for the good of the community. Since the community is the Body of Christ, each gift should be considered important for the life of this Body just as each part of a physical body is important for its life.

The most valuable gifts are not necessarily the most "spectacular," but those which build up the community and serve LOVE, the greatest gift.

5) QUESTIONS CONCERNING THE RESURRECTION OF THE BODY

Paul's Response:
There is an intimate connection between Christ's resurrection and the resurrection of our bodies. The resurrection will not be a return to the life we have known but a complete transformation of that which is corruptible to that which is incorruptible.

IMPORTANT NOTE:
In Paul's eyes, the Christian community is unique because it assumes Christ's own approach to life. Therefore, what a Christian believes should determine how a Christian behaves. To know Christ is to know how to act as a Christian. This principle should be the underlying factor in the Christian lifestyle.

2 CORINTHIANS

Occasion:
(around 57 A.D. from Macedonia)
Apparently rival missionaries have entered the community and are subverting Paul's work there. Paul speaks of a second visit he had made to Corinth and how during that time he experienced a very painful incident. This incident involved a questioning of the reality and nature of his apostolic mission. Questions arose concerning his motives, sincerity, weaknesses, and even the authenticity of his apostleship.

Principal Themes in 2 Corinthians:

1) THE QUESTIONING OF PAUL'S APOSTOLIC AUTHORITY

   Paul's Response:
   A true apostle (minister) receives his/her ministry through God's mercy, not through anything he/she does. The true apostle doesn't boast of accomplishments, but of weakness through which God's power can work. Thus, the mystery of Christ is lived out.

   Since the apostle is the link between the community and Christ, if the community questions the apostle's authenticity it is actually questioning its own authenticity. Therefore, Paul also defends his apostleship for the sake of the Corinthian Christian community.

2) GOD'S PLAN FOR "RECONCILIATION"

   God has reconciled an alienated world through Christ, not counting humanity's sins against it. God's people have been entrusted with the message of reconciliation and are called upon to be ambassadors for Christ in the exercise of this ministry.

3) THE COLLECTION FOR THE JERUSALEM CHURCH

   The collection being taken up for the Jerusalem church is important not only in that one church helps another, but also because it stands as a symbol of the breaking down of barriers between the Jewish Christian community and the Gentile Christian community.

IMPORTANT NOTE:
The truly emotional and personal Paul emerges in this letter. We see Paul's vulnerability, passion, love for his people, and the intensity of his convictions. Paul has deepened his understanding of a Christian apostle as one who is thoroughly identified with the cross of Christ rather than with any successful ministry from a human point of view.

GALATIANS

This letter is addressed to churches in an area rather than to a single community. It is a like a "circular" letter that each community is to read and pass on. Most likely it was written to the communities of northern Galatia, which were primarily Gentile.

Occasion:
(c. 54 or 57 A.D. from Ephesus or Macedonia)
Shortly after Paul's second visit to Galatia, different Christian missionaries came to the communities. These were primarily concerned with having Gen-

tiles adopt Jewish-Christian traditions (hence we often refer to them as "Judaizers"). They challenged both Paul's apostolic authority and his interpretation of the gospel. They claimed Paul had watered down the gospel message for Gentiles by neglecting the Mosaic Law. Evidently their doctrine of Christian salvation included continuing many of the practices of the Mosaic Law.

Principal Themes in Galatians:

Paul has learned that the Galatians were confused by the teaching of the Judaizers. He fears that the result will be a change from the gospel that he has preached. So he sends a very strong letter warning the communities against the "new"gospel. Insisting that his gospel is the genuine one, Paul emphasizes the freedom of Christians from the practices of the Mosaic Law. Paul also defends his apostolic authority because he knows that the community's faith depends upon this foundation.

Paul's View

1:1–2:21	In order to demonstrate the authenticity of his gospel, Paul gives documentation for his apostolic authority.
3:1–5:12	In Christ a new order has begun and there is now freedom from the Mosaic Law. Therefore the Galatians should not sacrifice their faith in Christ and revert back to the slavery of the Mosaic Law.
5:13–6:18	The authentic gospel which Paul preaches and the freedom it brings is not license to do anything one wants. Rather it is the source of all virtues and finally of everlasting life.

IMPORTANT NOTE:
In GALATIANS Paul emphasizes the freedom bestowed in Christ. Once there is true faith, the Christian embarks on the task of Christian living in response to God's gift of salvation. What this means is:

FREEDOM FROM:	1) the bondage of sin (whatever enslaves us or separates us from God)
	2) the burden of the Mosaic Law
FREEDOM FOR	life as children of God being heirs of eternal life empowerment by Holy Spirit transformation into the image of Christ

Paul is chiefly concerned with the freedom of those in Christ. Justification is Paul's way of describing God's saving activity in an argument about the ineffectiveness for salvation of the Mosaic Law.

ROMANS

Occasion:

(c. winter 57-58 A.D. from Corinth)
After much missionary activity in the eastern Mediterranean, Paul wishes to go to Spain. Prior to his departure from Corinth to carry the collection he has taken up to Jerusalem, he writes to the Romans to announce his plans to visit them. He wants to introduce himself to this church which he has not founded and thus does not know him personally. Paul presents his understanding of the gospel as a gift which he desires to leave with this church.

Although ROMANS reads more like a treatise than a letter, still it might very well address particular situations in the Roman community that Paul was aware of. Certainly, in either case it is a magnificently structured presentation of Paul's "gospel" as he had come to understand it after over twenty years of Christian ministry.

Principal Themes in Romans:

Paul believed that one's JUSTIFICATION and SANCTIFICATION depended not upon the practices (works) of the Mosaic Law, but rather on faith in Jesus Christ and incorporation by baptism into the death/resurrection experience. Through these, one shared in God's plan for salvation which had been achieved through Jesus Christ. Paul sketches out this basic theme in this way:

1. All humanity is alienated from God and thus in a state of sinfulness. Gentiles turn from God by not discovering God in the works of creation, and Jews break their special covenant relationship by not following the works of the Mosaic Law. In either case, the result is God's condemnation.

2. Humanity's attitude toward this alienation is crucial. If one adopts the attitude of self-sufficiency, that person takes the way to progressive wickedness, leading ultimately to death and the full experience of God's divine "wrath" (i.e. eternal separation from God).

3. But there is another way! God is a saving God who offers another possibility. If one abandons one's futile self-sufficiency and accepts the saving action of God through faith (basic trust, not the acceptance of a set of doctrines), then instead of the condemnation rightly deserved, God "justifies" the faithful person. God's saving action sets up the right relation of humanity to God. This sets the believer on the way to eternal life with God.

4. This journey to life is one of progressive sanctification. The toxic waste of sin is purified and the Holy Spirit is poured out into our hearts. God's love for us is the continuing guarantee that the continual work of sanctification will proceed to eternal life.

Other Themes:

Chapter 8 describes the magnificent role of the Holy Spirit in the dynamics of our Christian life.

The old Mosaic Law is replaced by the new law of the Spirit of life. Through the Holy Spirit God imparts to us something of God's own life so we can really live as God's children.

Baptism is highlighted not so much for its "washing from sin" as for its incorporation of the believer into Christ's death/resurrection experience. Through baptism we signify that we have "died" to the old way of relating to God and "live" now the right kind of relation which God has so generously offered us through Jesus Christ, who is always our model for genuine Christian living.

Paul agonizes over the refusal of the Jews to accept the Christian gospel. God has not been unfaithful to the covenant promises, so the fault must be their own. Paul believes that their failure has opened up the movement of God's salvation to the Gentiles. He is hopeful that the Jews will eventually accept the gospel and so be drawn into God's plan for the salvation of all humanity.

COLOSSIANS

There have been questions concerning the Pauline authorship of this letter due to:

1) differences in vocabulary from definitely Pauline letters

2) difference in style

3) more developed theology than found in the undisputed Pauline letters, e.g.
   - more elaborate theology of church (esp. church as body, Christ as head of the body)
   - God's plan of salvation as "mystery"
   - "cosmic" Christ

Scholars are divided on the issue of Pauline authorship. The majority appear to feel that Paul himself did not write this letter, but that it comes from a later time, perhaps the 80's A.D. or later. Paul had not founded this church. It was founded by his companion, Epaphras, and so maintains a Pauline spirit and influence.

COLOSSIANS is considered one of the "Captivity Letters." If it is genuinely Pauline, then it would most likely be dated to Paul's imprisonment in Rome (61-63 A.D.)

Occasion:

This letter is directed against false teachers. The exact nature of the errors being propagated is difficult to determine. The false teachers appear to be of a Jewish-Gnostic type who held:

1) a pseudo-philosophy; a wisdom other than the true gospel

2) a doctrine of angelic beings/"elemental spirits" in whom the fullness of the Godhead dwelt and upon whom creation depends (along with Christ, these must be worshipped by those seeking salvation.)

3) an asceticism with regard to eating and drinking, the necessity of ritual cleanness, and the observance of certain feasts and seasons.

For Paul, the principal error in all of this seems to be an implicit denial of the position of Christ as sole redeemer and mediator between the world of God and our human world.

Principal Themes in Colossians:

There is a very developed Christology which portrays Christ as:
    origin and head of ALL things and beings;
    the bringer of reconciliation;
    victor over all other powers through his cross;
      one in whom the fullness of God dwells;
    one in whom the entire world has all being,
      wisdom, knowledge and salvation;
    Head of his body, the church

IMPORTANT NOTE:
Paul makes use of an early christological hymn to emphasize and, in a sense, summarize his response (Col 1:15-20).

EPHESIANS

Serious questions, similar to those concerning the authorship of COLOSSIANS, have been raised about EPHESIANS. In addition, there is further complication due to the singular relationship between these two letters of which COLOSSIANS appears to be the original.

A majority of scripture scholars hold that EPHESIANS was not written by Paul, but comes from a much later date, e.g. 80's or later. If this is so, it is too bad that we do not know the identity of the author, because the author is a very profound theologian who takes Paul's own theological thinking to conclusions Paul did not make.

EPHESIANS is another of the "captivity letters" and if one accepts Pauline authorship, it would be dated 61-63 A.D.

Occasion:

Nothing in the letter itself indicates why this "doctrinal summary" was sent. Due to the relationship between this letter and COLOSSIANS, perhaps the rise of similar problems found at Colossae encouraged the author to compose EPHESIANS.

Principal Themes:

THE MYSTERY OF GOD'S PLAN FOR THE SALVATION OF ALL HUMANITY

— Achieved by the atoning death of Christ

— Manifested in the Church (the body) which has Christ as its Head.

THE WORLDWIDE CHURCH:

— Christ's body and his visible/tangible presence in the cosmos

— Become members through baptism and so participate in the saving mystery of Christ's death, resurrection, exaltation

— The faithful are not only beneficiaries of salvation, but also its instruments for others

— God's plan has been realized initially in Christ, and must be fully accomplished in the members of Christ's body (the Church) and in the whole of creation

IMPORTANT NOTE:
There are several factors which indicate that this letter was not originally addressed to the church at Ephesus alone:

> The detached tone of the letter, e.g. absence of personal greetings and references (remember that this church was founded by Paul and that he spent about three years there).

> The phrase "in Ephesus" (1:1) is not found in the earliest and best manuscripts (it apparently was added by a later hand).

One possible solution is that EPHESIANS was originally a "circular letter" sent to no one particular church community, but to several churches in the province of Asia, of which Ephesus was one.

PHILEMON

From among the genuinely Pauline letters which we have, this is the only personal letter from Paul to an individual rather than to a church community.

PHILEMON is another of Paul's "captivity letters," written from Rome around 61-63.

Occasion:

Philemon was a convert of Paul's from Colossae. This letter is concerned with Paul's meeting a certain Onesimus (this name means "useful") who turns out to be a runaway slave of Philemon. Paul has converted Onesimus to Christianity and originally wanted him to help in the Christian mission. But, Paul decides not to do anything without asking Philemon's permission first, since Philemon is still Onesimus' master. Paul chooses to return Onesimus to Philemon while suggesting in this letter that Philemon might now want to look upon his slave as a "brother in Christ."

Principal Themes:

Becoming a Christian changes the course of one's life and one's perspective on life. If Onesimus is considered a brother in faith, how would this affect both his life and that of Philemon?

Paul does not command Philemon to do anything. However, he does encourage Philemon to receive Onesimus back as a "brother," forgiving him any debt owed or injury caused.

What this letter does NOT seem to do is to attack the institution of slavery itself. Rather, it deals with the personal transformation which must take place within the Christian person, a transformation affecting all phases of one's life, especially those instances where the enslavement of others is very real.

23. IMAGES OF SALVATION USED BY PAUL

Paul understood that God had acted decisively for our salvation through the passion, death, burial, resurrection, exaltation and heavenly intercession of Jesus Christ. When Paul considered these events and what God had done through them, he used many different images to convey what God's saving action was like and what its effects on us were. Like a many-sided jewel, Paul sometimes gazed at this saving event in one way, and at other times he expressed it in a different way. The many images of salvation are derived both from Hellenistic and Jewish backgrounds. In understanding these images, we must consider their source or origin, their occurrence in Paul's letters, and finally the meaning that they have for Paul's proclamation of the Christian gospel.

IMAGE	SOURCE	FOUND IN	POINTS TOWARD GOD'S ACTION AS
SACRIFICE	LITURGY/ WORSHIP	1 COR 5:7	ACCEPTING CHRIST'S DEATH AS A SELF-OFFERING IN OBEDIENCE TO GOD'S WILL
EXPIATION	LITURGY/ WORSHIP	ROM 3:25	ERASING OUR GUILT BY THE SPRINKLING OF CHRIST'S BLOOD
SANCTIFICATION	LITURGY/ WORSHIP	1 COR 1:30; 6:11 1 THES 4:7	PURIFYING (WASHING) AND CONSECRATING US
REDEMPTION	SOCIAL RELATIONS	GAL 4:5 1 COR 6:20; 7:23	PAYING THE PRICE TO RANSOM US OR TO BUY OUR FREEDOM BACK FOR US
LIBERATION	SOCIAL RELATIONS	GAL 5:1, 13 2 COR 3:17 ROM 6:16-23	SETTING US FREE FROM SIN, DEATH, AND THE MOSAIC LAW, MAKES US NOW CITIZENS OF GOD'S "KINGDOM"
RECONCILIATION	HUMAN RELATIONS	2 COR 5:18-19 ROM 5:10-11 ROM 11:15	RESTORING A RELATIONSHIP OF FRIENDSHIP AND INTIMACY WHICH OUR SINFULNESS HAD BROKEN DOWN
SALVATION	MEDICAL HEALING	ROM 1:16 1 COR 1:18, 21	A HEALING, A RESTORATION OF HEALTH AFTER THE SICKNESS OF SIN
JUSTIFICATION	LEGAL/ JUDGMENT	ROM 3:21-28 GAL 2:15-21	A LEGAL ACQUITTAL DESPITE OUR SINFULNESS ACCORDING TO THE MOSAIC LAW
NEW CREATION	NATURE	2 COR 5:17 GAL 6:15	STARTING OF A COMPLETELY NEW REALITY
ADOPTION	FAMILY RELATIONS	ROM 8:15	GIVING MEMBERSHIP IN GOD'S NEW FAMILY
TRANSFORMATION	GROWTH & CHANGE	2 COR 3:18	CHANGING CHRISTIANS INTO LIVING IMAGES OF JESUS
GLORIFICATION	JEWISH THEOLOGY	ROM 8:30 1 THES 2:12	FILLING US WITH THE "GLORY" OR PRESENCE OF GOD JUST AS THE RISEN JESUS SHARES WITH GOD

24. HOUSE CHURCHES AND THE EUCHARIST

Jerome Murphy-O'Connor O.P.

House churches [were] the first type of sacred place for worship and prayer in earliest Christianity, the continuation of the "upstairs room" where Jesus ate the Passover supper with his disciples (Luke 22:12-14) and where, after his glorious ascension into heaven, the disciples gathered for prayer (Acts 1:12-14). Archaeology shows that at Corinth the triclinium and atrium take the place of the biblical "upstairs room." In the following article, Father Jerome Murphy-O'Connor provides many other, still more intriguing insights into the church situation at Corinth, its social divisions, and serious religious problems. Archaeology thus illustrates many passages of Paul's letters to the Corinthians. If we think further into the implications of the evidence, we may be led to new, challenging insights into church leadership through this reconstruction of an ancient city.

A Wealthy Roman Home at Corinth

Private houses were the first centers of church life. Christianity in the first century A.D., and for long afterward, did not have the status of a recognized religion, so there was no question of a public meeting-place, such as the Jewish synagogue. Hence, use had to be made of the only facilities available, namely, the dwellings of families that had become Christian.

Four houses of the Roman period have been brought to light at Corinth. Of these only one can be attributed to the time of Paul, the villa at Anaploga (Fig. 1). The magnificent mosaic floor of the triclinium (dining room) is dated to the late first century A.D., and broken pottery in the fill laid to provide a level bed comes from the period A.D. 50-75, but the building was already in existence when the mosaic was created.

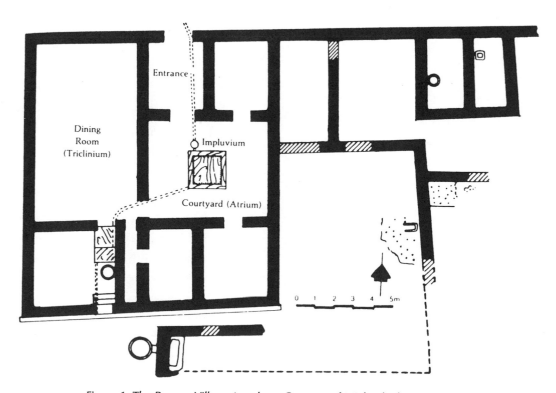

Figure 1. The Roman Villa at Anaploga. Courtesy of Michael Glazier, Inc.

Given the social conditions of the time, it can be assumed that any gathering which involved more than very intimate friends of the family would be limited to the public part of the house, and our concern here is to try and determine how much space was available. In the villa at Anaploga the triclinium measures 5.5 x 7.5 meters, giving a floor area of 41.25 sq. meters. This volume, however, would have been diminished by the couches around the walls; there would have been space for nine to recline. The atrium located just outside measures 5 x 6 meters, but the floor area of 30 sq. meters must be reduced also because at least one-ninth of the floor was taken up by the impluvium (from the Latin word *pluo,* to rain). This was a pool to collect the water that came through a hole of corresponding size in the roof; this was called the compluvium and was designed to light the atrium.

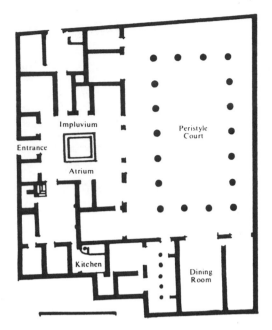

*Figure 2. House of the Vetii at Pompeii.
Courtesy of Michael Glazier, Inc.*

House Measurements and Number of Guests

These dimensions were very typical, as can be seen from a number of comparisons. "Another sumptuous villa of the second century has been excavated in the vicinity of the old Sicyonian Gate" (Wiseman, 1979: 528). The adjective used should be noted, together with the formulation which indicates that it also applies to the villa at Anaploga. The five magnificent mosaic floors were published by Shear (1925:391-397). No plan is given, but the dimensions of the rooms are provided: atrium, 7.15 x 7.15 = 51.12 sq. meters with a square impluvium in the center; triclinium off the atrium, 7.05 x 7.05 = 49.7 sq. meters. The excavator considers it probable that the mosaic floors were made before 146 B.C. and were simply incorporated when the villa was rebuilt in the second century A.D. The equally well-to-do House of the Vetii at Pompeii (Fig. 2), destroyed by the eruption of A.D. 79, was of similar size; the atrium was 7 x 6 = 42 sq. meters, and the triclinium 4 x 6.3 = 25.2 sq. meters. The consistency of such figures for upper-class houses can be seen from the

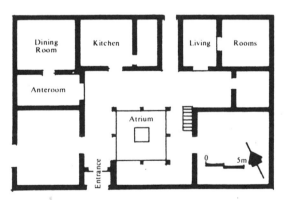

*Figure 3. Villa of Good Fortune at Olynthus.
Courtesy of Michael Glazier, Inc.*

dimensions of the fourth century B.C. Villa of Good Fortune at Olynthus (southeast of Thessalonica on the coast); the triclinium was 5.8 x 5 = 29 sq. meters, and the atrium with its impluvium 10 x 10 = 100 sq. meters (Fig. 3).

If we average out the floor areas for the four houses, the average size of the atrium is 55 sq. meters and that of the triclinium 36 sq. meters. Not all this area, however, was usable. The effective space in the triclinium was limited by the couches around the walls; the rooms surveyed would not have accommodated more than nine, and this is the usual number. The impluvium in the center of the atrium would not only have diminished the space by one-ninth, but would also have restricted movement; circulation was possible only around the outside of the square. Thus, the maximum number that the atrium could hold was fifty, but this assumes that there were no decorative urns, etc. to take up space, and that everyone stayed in one place; the true figure would probably be between thirty and forty.

The Christian Home of Gaius

Let us for a moment assume that this was the house of Gaius, a wealthy member of the Christian community at Corinth (Rom 16:23), and try to imagine the situation when he hosted "the whole church" (1 Cor 14:23). From Paul's letters we know the names of fourteen male members of the Corinthian community. We must suppose that, like Aquila, all were married. This brings us to twenty-eight persons, which is obviously the minimum figure. Neither Luke nor Paul intend to give a complete list; mentions of particular names were occasioned by specific circumstances. Moreover, we are told that the households of two members of the community, Crispus (Acts 18:8) and Stephanas (1 Cor 1:16; 16:15-16), were baptized with them. Thus, we have to add an indeterminate number of children, servants/slaves, and perhaps relations. It would be more realistic, therefore, to think in terms of around fifty persons as a base figure.

This number could barely be accommodated in our average house of Gaius, but it would have meant extremely uncomfortable overcrowding in the villa at Anaploga. It would appear, therefore, that a meeting of "the whole church" (Rom 16:23; 1 Cor 14:23) was exceptional; it would simply have been too awkward. Moreover, as Robert Banks has pointed out, the adjective "whole" is unnecessary if Corinthian Christians met only as a single group, and so must be understood to imply

that other groups existed. This observation suggests that the formulae "the whole church" and "the church in the house of X" (Rom 16:5; 1 Cor 16:19; Col 4:15; Phlm 2) should not be equated, but contrasted.

"The church in the house of X," then, would be a subgroup of the larger community. If Aquila and Priscilla/Prisca acted as the center of such a subgroup in Ephesus (1 Cor 16:19) and Rome (Rom 16:5), it is very probable that they did likewise in Corinth. Such subgroups would have been made up of the family, servants, and a few friends who lived in the vicinity. While such subgroups would have tended to foster an intimate family-type atmosphere, they would also have tended to promote divisions within the wider city community. It seems likely that the various groups mentioned by Paul (1 Cor 1:12—"I belong to Paul . . . to Apollos . . . [to] Cephas . . . to Christ") would regularly have met separately. Such relative isolation would have meant that each group had a chance to develop its own theology, and virtually ensured that it took good root before being confronted by other opinions.

The difficulty of getting the whole church together regularly in one place goes a long way toward explaining the theological divisions within the Corinthian community, but the difficulties of the physical environment also generated other problems when all the believers assembled as a church.

Class Distinctions of Wealthy and Poor

The mere fact that all could not be accommodated in the triclinium meant that there had to be an overflow into the atrium. It became imperative for the host to divide his guests into two categories; the first-class believers were invited into the triclinium while the rest stayed outside. Even a slight knowledge of human nature indicates the criterion used. The host must have been a wealthy member of the community, and so he invited into the triclinium his closest friends among the believers, who would have been of the same social class. The rest could take their places in the atrium, where conditions were greatly inferior. Those in the triclinium would have *reclined,* as was the custom (see 1 Cor 8:10) and as Jesus always did with his disciples, whereas those in the atrium were forced to *sit* (I Cor 14:30).

The space available made such discrimination unavoidable, but this would not diminish the resentment of those provided with second-class facilities. Here we see one possible source of the tensions that appear in Paul's account of the eucharistic liturgy at Corinth (1 Cor 11:17-34). However, his statement that "one is hungry while another is drunk" (v. 21) suggests that such tensions were probably exacerbated by another factor, namely, the type of food offered.

Since the Corinth that Paul knew had been refounded as a Roman colony in 44 B.C., and since Latin was the official language up to the end of the first century A.D., it is legitimate to assume that Roman customs enjoyed a certain vogue. One such custom was to serve different types of food to different categories of guests. Pliny the Younger recounts the following experience:

> I happened to be dining with a man, though no particular friend of his, whose elegant economy, as he called it, seemed to me a sort of stingy extravagance. The best dishes were set in front of himself and a select few, and cheap scraps of food before the rest of the company. He had even put the wine into tiny little flasks, divided into three categories, not with the idea of giving his guests the opportunity of choosing, but to make it impossible for them to refuse what they were given. One lot was intended for himself and for us, another for his lesser friends (all his friends are graded), and the third for his and our freedmen....
>
> (*Letters,* 2:6)

The same custom naturally proved fair game for the Roman satirists of the first century A.D. The entire Fifth Satire of Juvenal is a vicious dissection of the sadism of the host who makes his inferior guests "prisoners of the great smells of his kitchen" (line 162). With much greater brevity Martial makes the same point with equal effectiveness:

> Since I am asked to dinner, no longer, as before a purchased guest, why is not the same dinner served to me as to you? You take oysters fattened in the Lucrine lake, I suck a mussel through a hole in the shell. You get mushrooms, I take hog funguses. You tackle turbot, but I brill. Golden with fat, a turtledove gorges you with its bloated rump, but there is set before me a magpie that has died in its cage. Why do I dine without you, Ponticus, though I dine with you? The dole has gone: let us have the benefit of that; let us eat the same fare.
>
> (*Epigrams,* 3:60)

> We drink from glass, you from murrine, Ponticus. Why? That a transparent cup may not betray your two wines.
>
> (*Epigrams,* 4:85)

Only the wealthy are attracted by this method of saving, and it is entirely possible that a Corinthian believer, responsible for hosting the whole church, found it expedient to both demonstrate his sophistication and exercise financial prudence by serving different types of food to the two groups of believers — a distinction imposed on him by the physical arrangement of his house. Since the host's friends were of the leisured class, they could arrive early and feast on larger portions of superior food while awaiting the arrival of lower-class believers who were not as free to dispose of their time. The condition of those reclining gorged in the triclinium could hardly be disguised from those who had to sit in the atrium.

Many Members, One Body — with Christ
(1 Cor 12:12)

The reconstruction is hypothetical, but no scenario has been suggested which so well explains the details of 1 Corinthians 11:17-34. The admonition "wait for one another" (v. 34) means that *prolambanô* in v. 21 necessarily has a temporal connotation; some began to eat before others. Since these possessed houses with plenty to eat and drink (vv. 22, 34), they came from the wealthy section of the community and might have made a contribution in kind to the community meal. This, they felt, gave them the right to think of it as "theirs" (*to idion deiphon*). Reinforced by the Roman customs, they would then have considered it their due to appropriate the best portions for themselves. Such selfishness would necessarily include a tendency to take just a little more, so that it might happen that nothing was left for the "have-nots" (v. 22), who in their hunger had to content themselves with the bread and wine provided for the Eucharist. However, as Paul is at pains to point out, under such conditions no Eucharist is possible (v. 20).

Reprinted from *The Bible Today*, Vol. 22, No. 1 (January 1984), pp. 32-38.

25. WHAT THE CORINTHIANS SAID TO PAUL

If we remember that Paul is responding to specific problems of his communities, we can reconstruct the kind of things that the Corinthian community thought and said. These ideas and attitudes are attacked and criticized in Paul's response to them.

Is not the Christian religion primarily concerned with possessing the Holy Spirit and displaying the gifts of the Spirit in the worship service with uninhibited freedom (12:1–14:40)? All social and cultural restraints can now be tossed aside like a woman's veil, because we are free in Christ (11:2-16). And who can say what this freedom means for another? It is an individual matter. Some have quit sleeping with their spouses (7:1-7) because of their commitment to Christ, while another is living with his father's wife (5:1-8). Who is to judge? If there is a legal issue involved, go to court (6:1-8). But as for sex, marriage, and divorce, who is to say (7:1-39)? But maybe we do need to write to Paul and ask him these things (7:1).

Some in the church think we should break completely with the past, even to refusing meat which has been ritually offered to idols (8:1-13), but several of us have no problem with it. After all, meat is meat. Apparently some are not yet mature. In fact, it is a real question how much a letter from Paul will help us; he is not only quite conservative in his views on social issues, but on some things he is unreal! He keeps trying to get us all to the same table for fellowship and the Lord's Supper when the fact is, our different cultural and economic backgrounds really show up on social occasions (11:20-34).

The newer ministers champion liberty and make the gospel easy and clear. Who needs Paul's metaphors and paradoxes when a simple slogan will say it: "All things are lawful" (6:12, 10:23); "all possess knowledge " (8:1); "An idol has no real existence" (8:4); and "There is no God but one" (8:4). Paul always brings up the eschaton and the resurrection. Why all the future stuff when we are already rich and reigning here and now (4:8)? There is in our letter to Paul (7:1) a question about "the resurrection of the body," and no doubt we will get another of his long and confusing answers (15:12-58). But we do need help from someone; this church is tearing itself apart (11:18-19).

The three members who went to see Paul (16:17) should be returning soon, but they did not really need to go since Chloe sends somebody running to Paul (1:11) every time one of us sneezes. Personally, when ministers leave they should stay gone, period, and not keep writing back (5:9; 2 Cor 2:4), much less always promising (or threatening) to return (4:19-21; 2 Cor 1:15-22; 2 Cor 12:14-13:10). And sending us one of his helpers is useless (16:10-12): everyone knows associate ministers have no authority anyway.

Adapted from
Fred B. Craddock,
"Preaching to Corinthians,"
Interpretation 44 no. 2 (April 1990):160-161.

26. PAUL: SELF-QUIZ 1

ACTS, PAUL, 1 AND 2 THESSALONIANS, PHILIPPIANS, 1 AND 2 CORINTHIANS

1. Who is the author of ACTS?
    When was ACTS written?
    Where was the community located?
    Why did the author write ACTS?

2. In what city was Paul born?
    What was Paul's occupation or trade?
    To what Jewish "party" did Paul belong?
    Where did Paul's life-changing encounter with Christ occur?
    Why was he going there?
    According to Christian tradition, where did Paul die a martyr's death?

3. What do you consider to be Paul's most important contribution to the Church of his time?

4. What do you consider to be Paul's most important contribution for today's Church?

5. Give the approximate date of writing and the community situation for:
    1 THESSALONIANS
    2 THESSALONIANS (if Paul is author)
    PHILIPPIANS
    1 CORINTHIANS
    2 CORINTHIANS

6. What are the most important themes found in each of the following:
    ACTS
    1 THESSALONIANS
    2 THESSALONIANS
    PHILIPPIANS
    1 CORINTHIANS
    2 CORINTHIANS

7. Briefly explain the meaning of the greek term *"Kenosis"* as found in the hymn Paul uses in Philippians 2:7.

8. Briefly explain the meaning of the Greek term *"Parousia."*

27. SIX MORE LETTERS FROM ST. PAUL:

EXPLORING THE PAULINE HERITAGE

By Steve Mueller

Previously we examined six letters of St. Paul which all biblical scholars agree he wrote. Now we turn to six more letters commonly attributed to Paul but which, say many scholars, may not have actually come from his hand. These letters — often different from the others in literary or theological tone — are 2 Thessalonians, Colossians, Ephesians, and the three Pastoral letters — 1 Timothy, 2 Timothy and Titus.

When we discuss the immediate authorship of these letters, however, we are not intimating that they do not belong to the deposit of faith. They are divinely revealed and inspired revelation. And if not written by Paul himself, they were likely written by his followers. Moreover, they have shaped the Pauline tradition after his death. Indeed, they extend Paul's own teachings by applying them to new situations confronting the Church.

Our task is not to get bogged down in debates about authorship but to probe the message of these writings. The best way to do this is actually to read the letters. So, be sure to have your New Testament at hand. This article is designed to guide and serve you as you explore the challenging terrain of the Pauline heritage.

Seeing Paul as a Model:
Persuading through Example

Paul, or his followers, didn't write their letters just to impart information about Christian doctrine. They wanted to persuade people to change their minds, to change their lives. So we shall focus on the way each letter tries to persuade us to live as Christians.

The main method of persuasion is not logical arguments, as we might suspect, but models for imitation. Each letter chooses a certain portrait of Paul which exemplifies the beliefs and behaviors which the community ought to adopt.

Second Thessalonians:
The Apocalyptic Paul

All Christians believed that a new age had begun with Jesus. They thought that this new creation would begin soon after his resurrection, or at least in their lifetime when Jesus would return again in glory. First they expected a violent end to their world, then the beginning of a glorious new epoch. The imaginative picture of how this end and beginning might occur was found in a stylized type of writing called apocalyptic (from the Greek word for "revelation"). The Book of Revelation (sometimes called The Apocalypse) is the classic Christian example of this style of writing. It can also be found in Jesus' discourses about the destruction of the Jerusalem temple and the end of the world in Mark 13, Matthew 24–26, and Luke 21.

We recall how Paul's first letter to the Thessalonians addressed their difficulties with his teaching about the end-time. Paul's emphasis was not on when the world might end but on how we are to live each day in a Christian way. The second letter to the Thessalonians returns to this problem.

If not written by Paul himself, it was most likely written shortly after the martyrdom of Paul (in 67 or 68 according to Christian tradition). At this time, Christians were undergoing their first taste of persecution in Rome because Nero had blamed them for burning the city in 64. In the Holy Land, Christians were caught in the war that Jewish zealots had launched against the Roman occupying forces. For many Christians, the end of the world seemed at hand.

The opening of the letter (1:1-10) encourages the community in the face of their persecution. Paul assures them that God will punish their persecutors when Jesus returns in glory. The mention of this second coming introduces the main argument of the letter in chapter 2.

The Thessalonians have been upset by people claiming that the end has already come. But Paul argues that this cannot be true. The events which must happen before the end occurs have not yet taken place. Neither the "rebellion" (apostasy) nor the revelation of "the lawless one" has occurred. Some mysterious force (the "what" of verse 6) and some powerful person (the "who" of verse 7) are now temporarily restraining him.

Still to come is the great cosmic battle in which this lawless one who is guided by Satan (2:9) will be conquered by the Lord Jesus (2:8). The images Paul is using here represent standard Jewish ideas about the process for the end of the world as found, for example, in the Book of Daniel, chapters 7-12.

But Paul mostly wants to shift the Thessalonians' concern from the end-time to the present time — to Christian life in this world. He reminds them that God has chosen them and called them so that they can also be with the risen Christ (2:13-14). But their salvation depends on the way they now live.

In the final chapter, since Paul is not working up to a logical conclusion, he instead encourages the Thessalonians to be courageous despite their persecutions (3:1-5). Next, Paul uses himself as a model for their behavior. The "disorderly" troublemakers, who do not do their share of the work but expect the community to care for them, are challenged by the image of Paul as an "orderly" person who worked hard and did not disrupt the community (3:6-16).

Our reading of 2 Thessalonians reveals the author's concern to revive the earliest image of Paul as champion of the apocalyptic approach within Christianity. By offering this model of Paul for imitation, it is trying to persuade us that this apocalyptic Paul is the most authoritative Paul. And if this is the real Paul, then the Pauline churches ought to return to their apocalyptic roots. As they await the approaching end, they must live their Christian lives facing their present persecution rather than wasting time in useless speculation about the future.

Colossians:
The Cosmic Paul

As Christianity emerged in the last third of the first century into confrontation with the Hellenistic culture, it had to show that the "word of truth, the gospel" (1:5) provided a better basis for living than its pagan competitors, the "seductive philosophy of human traditions" (2:8). Instead of a perverse and capricious Fate which determined everyone's destiny, Christianity offered hope for a better life through faith in Jesus as Lord.

Where 2 Thessalonians tried to persuade us that the apocalyptic Paul is the real Paul, Colossians portrays Paul as a great Christian philosopher — the privileged recipient and wise interpreter of the mystery of God's revelation — who explains the Lordship of Christ over all creation and the effects of this Lordship on us.

The letter to the Colossians addresses a community which was challenged by the religious ideas of its Hellenistic neighbors. Because most people at this time experienced their world as a dangerous place controlled by hostile and terrifying powers, they turned to religion for security. People sought control through astrological charts, oracles, sacrifices, and mystery cults which promised knowledge of the secrets of life.

Apparently the pastor of the Colossian community, Epaphras, lacked the expertise to solve their problems. So he asked Paul to write from prison (4:3, 18) to help. Paul's letter outlines the Christian view of all reality under the Lordship of Christ and how we are to live as Christians.

After a brief introduction of himself as an apostle and a prayer for increased spiritual wisdom, Paul offers a theological teaching on Christ's place in the universal framework of creation (1:15-2:3). Jesus — instead of "Fate" or any other power — is the Lord over all. Paul uses a beautiful Christian hymn (1:15-20) to review the whole course of Christ's saving work. Christ's Lordship over all creation includes his headship over the Church, which is identified as his body.

Then Paul illustrates how Christ's saving work has been extended to us. Through him we have been brought into a new relationship with God. Paul's own life is the best example of how Christ's grace changes us. Although Paul suffers often as a minister of the gospel (1:23), he knows that his teaching and preaching, *together with his sufferings*, are linked to the greater mystery of Christ's death and resurrection as it is still being worked out in our world. Our lives are the place where God's salvation is now happening.

Paul next warns about false teachers who propose other viewpoints (2:4-20). This section is somewhat hard to understand because we cannot clearly identify either the false teachers or the ideas they propose.

But the thrust of the argument is clear. Christ is "the Lord" (2:6) and "the reality" (2:17) of our lives. We cannot substitute any other reality as lord or master of our lives, e.g. "the elemental powers of the world" (2:8, 20), "principalities or powers" (2:10, 15), or "worship of angels" (2:18). Nor can Christians trust in practices which result from these false ideas, such as special diets or horoscopes which tell us when to do things (2:16).

In the last section (2:20–4:6), Paul again concludes with an exhortation. The lifestyle of the false teachers contrasts sharply with the genuine Christian life. The Christian life is a dying to the world's power (2:20-23; 3:5-11) and rising with Christ (3:1-4; 12-17).

Paul includes here a standard list of duties (called "household codes") for wives/husbands,

children/parents, slaves/masters (3:18–4:1). These household codes reflect the rigid social status typical of the Hellenistic society. The duties expected of the "lower" rank are given first, followed by those of the "higher." Paul's use of these "household codes" reminds us that his views on moral behavior were greatly conditioned by the culture of his time. But we also note that Paul does not always accept these Hellenistic expectations at face value. He often "Christianizes" them by giving new reasons for doing what was already expected in the Hellenistic world.

Ephesians:
The Ecclesial Paul

The Letter to the Ephesians invokes Paul's authority to deal with disunity in the Church. During Paul's lifetime, the struggle had been to let Gentiles into the primarily Jewish-Christian Church. Paul was so successful that by the 80's the Church was predominantly Gentile-Christian. Now Jewish Christians found it difficult to find a place in the newly Hellenized Church. But, as Matthew's gospel (written about 85) indicates, they did it.

In this letter, Paul's authority is used to stress the universal unity which joins the many local churches. The worldwide character of the Church preoccupies Paul. If Paul's missionary work had contributed to the growing disunity, then this letter eloquently reminds Gentile Christians of the greater unity of the worldwide ("catholic") Church. This letter reads like a meditation on Church unity.

Paul begins by reminding them that both for him as an apostle and for them as a community, their unity is founded on their common relation to God. Each has been elected and lovingly called by God the Father to experience redemption through adoption into Christ and sealing in the Holy Spirit (1:1-14).

Next Paul prays that they might recognize Christ's universal Lordship over all creation and over the Church, which is his body (1:15-23). Not only are we unified because we have one Lord, but also because our association with Christ has changed us. Since we all — both Gentile and Jew — have been transformed from death in sin to life in Christ, we belong to one new family — "the household of God" which is also a sacred temple where God now dwells (2:1-22).

Paul then points out that we are also unified in our mission to bring about the fullness of God's plan of salvation for the whole world (3:1-13). "When you read this," he writes, "you will understand my insight into the mystery of Christ" (3:4). He prays that we might experience God's unifying love (3:14-21) and notes the sevenfold bonds of unity which hold us together — "one body and one Spirit, as you were also called to the one hope of your call; one Lord, one faith, one baptism; one God and Father of all" (4:4-6).

Although united into one community, we still retain our personal gifts as apostles, prophets, evangelists, pastors and teachers. These gifts equip us for our ministry and for building up the unity of the body of Christ (4:7-16).

As we might expect, the remainder of the letter (4:17–6:23) spells out the kind of new behavior which we must have in order to be "living the truth in love" (4:17). We must imitate God and live in love (5:1-20) in order to transform ourselves and the world we live in. Our behavior will be very different if we live in the light of goodness and truth.

Paul again introduces the "household codes" (5:21–6:9) with their hierarchical relationships. But now he shows how Christian love changes the expected behavior of husbands to their wives, parents to their children, and masters to their slaves. Of particular interest here is Paul's attempt to supply Christian reasons for husbands to love their wives.

Since love was not part of their cultural expectations of family-arranged marriages, Paul uses various arguments to change the Christian husband's attitude. First he appeals to Christ's love

for the Church as model (5:25-27). Since this might not be very convincing, Paul then appeals to their own self-love (5:28-29). He next compares marriage to the mysterious relationship of Christ to the Church (5:29-31). This lengthy attempt to change the husband's attitude shows how different their expectations about marriage were from our own.

In this letter Paul is portrayed as an apostle (1:1) and a prisoner (3:1, 4:1, 6:20). Yet his primary importance emerges in another way. As the steward of the mystery of Christ, he plays a major role in the drama of salvation as it has been revealed to him (1:7-9; 3:1-13). For Paul, the unity of the Christian Church is the greatest visible sign that God's plan for the salvation of all humanity is already being achieved.

The Pastorals:
The Presence of the Absent Paul

The Pastorals are the latest Pauline letters. Probably written near the end of the first century, they claim Paul's authority for the growing institutionalization of the Church. These letters have always been grouped together (they might even have been written as a group), and are best read in the order of 1 Timothy, Titus, and 2 Timothy.

These letters contain Paul's advice for establishing similar administrative and pastoral traditions both for communities which he had founded (Timothy in Ephesus) and for communities which he did not found (Titus on Crete).

Paul is portrayed as an aging pastor whose final care for the community is expressed by appointing successors to continue his work. Throughout his ministry, Paul had often relied on his fellow-workers Timothy and Titus to speak and act for him in his absence. (See 1 Thessalonians 3:2, Galatians 2:1, 1 and 2 Corinthians.)

To these successors, Paul gives advice about some problems found in leading a large Christian community. The Church is now identified primarily as the "household of God" rather than the Body of

Christ. As a household, the Church is identified with the basic social and economic unit in the Hellenistic world. The emphasis is on the Church as a structured institution to which everyone could belong. The Church is both a home and a family.

This change also hints at the type of person who is needed to be a leader (1 Tim 3:1-13). Although we call them "pastors," the job description clearly calls not for a shepherd but for a manager — an *episkopos* (the root of our word "bishop"), the Greek word for the overseer of a household.

In 1 Timothy, Paul's advice to the younger man covers many different topics. But he constantly emphasizes Timothy's role as a teacher who must be on guard against false doctrine (1:3-11, 18-20; 4:1-5; 6:3-16). The tendency then (and now!) was to make Christianity into a set of interesting intellectual ideas with little application to everyday living. The primary false teaching is that Christian belief does not lead to action which transforms us and our world.

Paul also stresses the qualities necessary for authentic ministers in the community. Just as Paul's life is the archetype or model (1:15) of God's grace at work to change us, so Timothy's life continues the chain of imitation. He in turn must seek out others to assist him in his duties of prayer (2:1-15), teaching (4:6-16) and administration (5:1-6:2) so that what is entrusted to him can be passed on.

In the letter to Titus, Paul advises Titus about the qualities of the leaders — the "presbyter-bishops" (although these words will later distinguish priests and bishops, in this letter they are interchangeable), which Titus is to appoint for each town (1:5-9). He next describes the guidelines for Christian behavior for members of the community (2:1–3:11).

2 Timothy is Paul's personal farewell to Timothy. Along with the warnings against false teaching, Paul provides encouragement by drawing on his experience of being called to share in God's mysterious plan. Despite his sufferings and his loneliness, Paul is not discouraged and bitter. He is the living example for his final plea that Timothy "Be self-possessed in all circumstances, put up with hardship, perform the work of an evangelist, fulfill your ministry" (2 Tim 4:5).

Paul for Our Day:
New Problems, New Solutions

Having read these letters, we cannot help but note how similar Paul's situation is to our own. The Christian Church is still struggling to discover authentic applications of the gospel message for our times. These letters can aid our search for suitable answers to the complex problems of our own day.

First of all, these letters remind us of the importance of models. The greatest inspiration for living our Christian faith is not a clear statement of doctrine but a living example of Christian faith. Not only famous people like Mother Teresa or Bishop Romero, but especially the genuine saints who grace our everyday lives are the main reasons we keep trying to be good Catholics.

Second, these letters remind us of the overwhelming importance of our own "NOW." Countering the tendency to get lost in the triumphalism of our glorious past or overcome by the fears of an uncertain future, the letters remind us that God is working in our present lives to transform us and our world. If our lives are not changed, then we know our Christianity is not working.

Finally, these letters remind us that, as Vatican II so often put it, the Church is in the world. The Church is not separated from our everyday lives. Nor is the Church isolated from the many different cultures which girdle our earth. The Church must discover a way to embrace what is valuable in every culture and to criticize what is not in harmony with the Christian message. But Vatican II also notes, as Paul knew well, that the task starts first with ourselves.

"Such a mission requires us first of all to create in the Church itself mutual esteem, reverence and harmony, and acknowledge all legitimate diversity;...For the ties that unite the faithful together are stronger than those which separate them; let there be unity in what is necessary, freedom in what is doubtful, and charity in everything."
(*The Church in the Modern World*, # 92)

28. PAUL: SELF-QUIZ 2

GALATIANS, ROMANS, COLOSSIANS, EPHESIANS, PHILEMON

1.   Give the approximate date of writing and community situation for:

GALATIANS

ROMANS

COLOSSIANS

EPHESIANS

PHILEMON

2.   What are the most important themes found in:

GALATIANS

ROMANS

COLOSSIANS

EPHESIANS

PHILEMON

3.   What is the meaning of the following terms as *Paul* used them:

JUSTIFICATION

SANCTIFICATION

29. PAUL: SELF-QUIZ 3

1. Often thought to be Paul's favorite community based on his letter to them.   _____
2. Paul's "angry" letter.   _____
3. The shortest complete letter that we have of Paul's.   _____
4. The letter which is often called Paul's "Gospel."   _____
5. The letter which refers to Paul's appearance at the Council of Jerusalem.   _____
6. Paul's "captivity" letters.   _____
7. A letter we studied which was most likely not written by Paul himself.   _____

FROM WHAT LETTERS DO THE FOLLOWING QUOTES COME?

8. _____ "God was reconciling the world to himself in Christ, not counting their trespasses against them and entrusting to us the message of reconciliation."

9. _____ "I have been crucified with Christ; yet I live, no longer I, but Christ lives in me; insofar as I now live in the flesh, I live by faith in the Son of God who has loved me and given himself up for me."

10. _____ "Concerning times and seasons you have no need for anything to be written to you. For you yourselves know very well that the Day of the Lord will come like a thief at night."

11. _____ "For Jews demand signs and Greeks look for wisdom, but we proclaim Christ crucified, a stumbling block to Jews and foolishness to Gentiles, but to those who are called, Jews and Greeks alike, Christ the power of God and the wisdom of God."

12. _____ "For I am not ashamed of the gospel. It is the power of God for the salvation of everyone who believes: for Jew first, and then Greek."

13. _____ "...that at the name of Jesus every knee should bend, of those in heaven and on earth and under the earth, and every tongue confess that Jesus Christ is Lord, to the glory of God the Father."

14. _____ "I am sending Tychichus to you...so that you may know about us and that he may encourage your hearts, together with Onesimus, a trustworthy and beloved brother."

15. _____ "Three times I begged the Lord about this, that it might leave me, but he said 'My grace is sufficient for you, for power is made perfect in weakness.' I will gladly boast of my weakness."

16. _____ "For if the dead are not raised, neither has Christ been raised, and if Christ has not been raised, your faith is in vain: you are still in your sins."

17. _____ "For I am convinced that neither death, nor life, nor angels, nor principalities, nor present things, nor future things, nor powers, nor height, nor depth, nor any other creature will be able to separate us from the love of God in Christ Jesus our Lord."

18. _____ "But we hold this treasure in earthen vessels, that the surpassing power may be of God and not from us."

19. _____ "...one body and one Spirit...the one hope of your call; one Lord, one faith, one Baptism; one God and Father of all..."

20. Bonus: "The one instructed in the word should share all good things with the instructor."

Answers on next page

Answers to Self-Quiz on Paul's Letters

1. Philippians
2. Galatians
3. Philemon
4. Romans
5. Galatians
6. Philippians, Philemon, Colossians, Ephesians
7. Ephesians

Quotes:

8. 2 Corinthians 5:19
9. Galatians 2:19-20
10. 1 Thessalonians 5:2
11. 1 Corinthians 1:22-24
12. Romans 1:16
13. Philippians 2:10-11
14. Colossians 4:7-9
15. 2 Corinthians 12:8-9
16. 1 Corinthians 15:16-17
17. Romans 8:38-39
18. 2 Corinthians 4:7
19. Ephesians 4:4-6
20. Bonus: Galatians 6:6

30. THE HISTORY OF THE JOHANNINE COMMUNITY

PHASE ONE:
ORIGINS
(mid-50s to
late 80s)

ORIGINATING GROUP: In or near Palestine, Jews of relatively standard expectations, including followers of JBap, accepted Jesus without difficulty as the Davidic Messiah, the fulfiller of the prophecies, and one confirmed by miracles. Among this group was a man who had known Jesus during the ministry and who would become the Beloved Disciple.

SECOND GROUP: Jews of an anti-Temple bias who believed in Jesus and made converts in Samaria. They understood Jesus against a Mosaic rather than a Davidic background. He had been with God, seen him, and brought down his words to people.

The acceptance of the Second group catalyzed the development of a high, pre-existence christology, which led to debates with Jews who thought the Johannine community was abandoning Jewish monotheism by making a second God out of Jesus. Ultimately the leaders of these Jews had the Johannine Christians expelled from the synagogues. The latter, alienated from their own, saw "the Jews" as children of the devil. They stressed a realization of the eschatological promises in Jesus to compensate for what they had lost in Judaism. The Disciple made this transition and helped others to make it, thus becoming the Beloved Disciple.

GENTILE CONVERTS

PHASE TWO:
GOSPEL
(ca. 90)

Since the Jews were blinded, the coming of the Greeks was God's plan of fulfillment. The community may have moved from Palestine to the Diaspora to teach the Greeks. This contact brought out the universalistic possibilities in Johannine thought. However, rejection by others and persecution by "the Jews" convinced Johannine Christians that the world was opposed to Jesus, and that they should not belong to this world which was under the power of Satan. Rejection of the high Johannine christology by Jewish Christians was seen as unbelief and led to a breaking of communion (*koinōnia*). Communications were kept open to the Apostolic Christians (see page 138) with hopes for unity, despite differences of christology and church structure.

The defensive concentration on christology against "the Jews" and the Jewish Christians led to a split within the Johannine community.

PHASE THREE:
EPISTLES
(ca. 100)

THE ADHERENTS OF THE AUTHOR OF THE EPISTLES: To be a child of God one must confess Jesus come in the flesh and must keep the commandments. The secessionists are the children of the devil and the antichrists. The anointing with the Spirit obviates the need for human teachers: test all who claim to have the Spirit.

THE SECESSIONISTS: The One who has come down from above is so divine he is not fully human; he does not belong to the world. Neither his life on earth nor that of the believer has salvific import. Knowledge that God's Son came into the world is all important, and those who believe in this are already saved.

PHASE FOUR:
AFTER THE EPISTLES
(2nd century)

UNION WITH THE GREAT CHURCH: Unable to combat the secessionists simply by appealing to tradition, and losing out to their opponents, some of the author's adherents accepted the need for authoritative official teachers (presbyter-bishops). At the same time "the church catholic" showed itself open to the high Johannine christology. There was a gradual assimilation into the Great Church which was slow, however, to accept the Fourth Gospel since it was being misused by gnostics.

ROAD TO GNOSTICISM: The larger part of the Johannine community seems to have accepted secessionist theology which, having been cut off from the moderates through schism, moved toward true docetism (from a not fully human Jesus to a mere appearance of humanity), toward gnosticism (from a pre-existent Jesus to pre-existent believers who also came down from the heavenly regions), and toward Montanism (from possessing the Paraclete to the embodiment of the Paraclete). They took the Fourth Gospel with them; it was accepted early by gnostics who commented on it.

From Raymond Brown, *The Community of the Beloved Disciple* (New York: Paulist, 1979), pp. 166-167.

31. CHARACTERISTIC STYLE AND VOCABULARY: GOSPEL ACCORDING TO JOHN

(Summarized from Raymond Brown, *The Gospel According to John*; New York: Doubleday and Co., 1966, pp. cxxxv-cxxxvi.)

I. NOTABLE CHARACTERISTICS IN JOHANNINE STYLE

1.   **INCLUSION:** At the end of a passage, the gospel will often mention a detail or make an allusion which recalls something recorded in the opening of the passage. This feature will therefore "package" a unit by tying together the beginning and the end (e.g. 2:11 and 4:46,54: two Cana miracles).

2.   **CHIASM** (inverted parallelism): In two units which share a number of parallel features, the first verse of the first unit corresponds to the last verse of the second unit, the second verse of the first unit corresponds to the second-to-the-last verse of the second unit, etc. (e.g. 6:36,40 and 18:28, 19:16).

3.   **DOUBLE MEANING:** The gospel often plays on the double meaning of words in order to lead eventually to the "deeper" meaning (e.g. 3:3ff, "from above" and "again"; 4:10,11, "living" and "flowing"; 7:8, ambiguity of "going up" (to Jerusalem or to the Father).

4.   **MISUNDERSTANDING:** This feature is sometimes the counterpart to the twofold or double meaning.

In other instances, it is related to the symbolic language of Jesus. When Jesus is speaking on the heavenly or eternal level, his remarks are often misunderstood as referring to a material or earthly level/situation. This, then, gives Jesus the opportunity to further explain himself and move the one who "misunderstands" to a deeper level of insight/understanding.

5.   **IRONY:** The opponents of Jesus are often making statements about him which are derogatory, sarcastic, incredulous, or at least, inadequate in the sense they intend. However, by way of irony, these statements are often true or more meaningful in a sense they do not realize (e.g. 4:12; 7:35,42; 8:22; 11:50).

6.   **EXPLANATORY NOTES:** In this gospel, we often find explanatory comments inserted into the running narrative of the story. They explain names (1:38,42) and symbols (2:21; 7:33; 18:9); they correct possible misapprehensions (4:2; 6:6); they remind the reader of related events (3:24; 11:2) and reidentify for the reader the characters of the plot (7:50; 21:20). One scholar has identified some 59 such notes in John.

II. DUALISTIC PARALLELS IN JOHN

1.   **LIGHT/DARKNESS:** In John, *light* signifies the revelation of the Father in Christ which is apprehended by faith and which calls for moral activity in the believer. *Darkness* is the absence of this revelation which characterizes the "world" and those without faith and implies moral failure.

2.   **TRUTH/FALSEHOOD:** *Truth,* in John, refers to the total and definitive revelation of the Father made in Christ, precisely in the sphere of human activity and experience, which the Spirit makes effective in the believer so that it becomes the principle of the believer's life. *Falsehood* is not only the absence of this revelation, but opposition to it, rejection of it, or failure to live according to its demands (TRUTH/FALSEHOOD name the reality of the revelation and the opposition to it, while LIGHT/DARKNESS represent the same reality symbolically).

3.   **LIFE/DEATH:** *Life,* in John, designates eternal life, which is present in Jesus himself. It is communicated by him to those who accept him "in the present" and this acceptance is through faith. *Death* is the ultimate loss of this life. Life is the content of Truth (revelation) symbolized by Light, while Death is the content of Falsehood symbolized by Darkness.

III. JOHANNINE VOCABULARY

1. **WORLD:** Characteristically, in John, "world" applies to the world of human experience, the theater of salvation history, humanity, fallen creation. It often has a pejorative significance. Yet, it is clear that the "world" has not become evil in itself; rather it is oriented and dominated by evil. The "world" is consistently identified with those who have turned against Jesus, under the leadership of Satan. Yet, the "world" is also object of God's love. It is as savior of the "world" that Jesus comes, taking away its sins, and giving it life. In a sense, this recalls it from its situation as "world" (as described above).

2. **JUDGMENT:** In the NT, this word indicates condemnation to separation uttered against those who fall away from the design of God. Generally, in the NT, this judgment is reserved for the final times. Although present in John this way, "judgment" is already present in the person of Jesus in John. The purpose of Jesus' appearance is not to judge but to save. Nevertheless, his very appearance in the world is "judgment" upon those who reject him in disbelief; for those who accept him in faith, there is no "judgment."

3. **REVELATION:** For John, this means primarily the manifestation of the person of Jesus as Messiah and Son of God in the sphere of human experience. He is the manifestation of the Father. In this "revelation," the design of God for humankind is apparent, for it can be grasped in faith and love.

4. **GLORY:** The NT sense of this term comes from the OT usage, referring to the visible manifestation of God, usually in fire or smoke. In the NT, this idea expresses the divine manner of being (e.g. in power, etc.), applied not only to God, but also to Jesus. In John, this "glory" is applied to the earthly Jesus; in the rest of the NT, it is applied to the Risen Lord. This glory of Jesus is visible only to the eyes of faith and is demonstrated even in the cross.

5. **SIGN:** Characteristically, in John, "sign" is a great miracle of Jesus described in some detail. However, it is not precisely the miracle itself which is stressed by the evangelist, but the capacity of the "sign" to indicate the true character of Jesus as Messiah and Son of God. In this sense, the "sign" can be understood correctly only by faith.

6. **WORK:** The concept of "works" is both connected with and wider than that of miracle. Not only are Jesus' miracles "works," his words are "works" as well. The whole ministry of Jesus can be summed up by his "work." The "works" of Jesus are, therefore, the varied activities of his ministry (whether miraculous or not) which show him for who/what he is.

7. **FAITH:** "Faith" is of central importance. It runs through the whole gospel. The evangelist's purpose in writing is to generate faith which gives life. The noun for "faith" never occurs in John; instead John uses the verb "to believe." This emphasizes an active commitment to a person, in particular, to Jesus. Much more than trust or confidence, it is an acceptance of Jesus and what he claims to be, a dedication of one's life to him. This involves a willingness to respond to God's demands as they are presented in and by Jesus. This "faith" results in life.

8. **LOVE:** Again, John prefers the verb form rather than the noun form of this word. "Love" is the greatest and most characteristic of the Christian virtues. The source of this "love" is the Father, who lavishes it on the incarnate Son, and from the Son, it comes to the believer. This makes it incumbent for the believer to love his/her fellow believers, so that love for each other in John is emphasized more than the love of humankind for God and Christ. Love is inseparable from union with Christ and through him with God, a major theme of John. Not to "love" is to abide in death, but the one who loves has passed from death to life.

9. **REMAIN ("abide" "dwell in" "stay"):** This expresses the permanency of relationship between Father and Son and between Son and Christian. Divine indwelling is an intimate union that expresses itself in a way of life lived in love. To "remain" in Jesus, or in the Father, or in one of the divine gifts, is intimately associated with keeping the commandments in a spirit of love, with a struggle against the world, and with bearing fruit ... all basic Christian duties. Thus, indwelling is not the exclusive experience of chosen souls within the Christian community. It is the essential principle of all Christian life.

10. **HOUR:** In the synoptics, the word "hour" almost always refers to the hour of the day. John frequently uses the word to designate a particular and significant period in Jesus' life. John uses this term to especially refer to the "hour" of Jesus' return to the Father which is accomplished in passion, death, and resurrection (extending from Palm Sunday to Easter Sunday).

32. JEWISH CALENDAR AND SPECIAL FEAST DAYS

JEWISH CALENDAR

SACRED YEAR	CIVIL YEAR	HEBREW MONTH	WESTERN CORRELATION	FARM SEASONS	RELIGIOUS FEASTS
1	7	NISAN	MARCH - APRIL	BARLEY HARVEST	14 — PASSOVER 21 — FIRST FRUITS
2	8	LYYAR	APRIL - MAY	GENERAL HARVEST	
3	9	SIVAN	MAY - JUNE	WHEAT HARVEST VINE TENDING	6 — PENTECOST
4	10	TAMMUZ	JUNE - JULY	FIRST GRAPES	
5	11	AB	JULY - AUGUST	GRAPES, FIGS OLIVES	9 — DESTRUCTION OF TEMPLE
6	12	ELUL	AUGUST - SEPTEMBER	VINTAGE	
7	1	TISHRI	SEPTEMBER - OCTOBER	FRUIT & GRAPE HARVEST PLOUGHING	10 — YOM KIPPUR 15-21 — TABERNACLES
8	2	MARCHESVAN	OCTOBER - NOVEMBER	GRAIN PLANTING	
9	3	KISLEV	NOVEMBER - DECEMBER		25 — DEDICATION
10	4	TEBET	DECEMBER - JANUARY	RAINY SEASON SPRING GROWTH	
11	5	SHEBAT	JANUARY - FEBRUARY	WINTER FIGS	
12	6	ADAR	FEBRUARY - MARCH	PULLING FLAX ALMONDS BLOSSOM	13-14 — PURIM
		ADAR SHENI	INTERCALARY MONTH		

JEWISH SPECIAL FEAST DAYS

FEAST DAYS	HEBREW NAME	DAY	REFERENCE	READING (MEGILLOTH)	COMMEMORATION
PASSOVER	PESACH	14 NISAN	EXODUS 12 (LEV 23:4-8)	SONG OF SOLOMON	DELIVERANCE FROM EGYPT
PENTECOST	SHAVUOTH	6 SIVAN	DEUT 16:9-12 (LEV 23:9-14)	RUTH	CELEBRATION OF WHEAT HAR-VEST GIVING OF SINAI COVENANT
9TH OF AB	TISH'AH BE'AB	9 AB	NO DIRECT REFERENCE	LAMENTATIONS	DESTRUCTION OF JERUSALEM TEMPLE (586 B.C. AND 70 A.D.)
DAY OF ATONEMENT	YOM KIPPUR	10 TISHRI	LEV 16 (23:26-32)		SACRIFICES FOR SINS OF THE PEOPLE
FEAST OF TABERNACLES	SUCCOTH	15-21 TISHRI	NEH 8 LEV 23:33-36 JOHN 7:2	ECCLESIASTES	WANDERINGS IN THE WILDER-NESS (ALSO GRAPE AND FRUIT HARVEST FEAST)
DEDICATION	CHANUKAH	25 KISLEV	1 MC 4:36,59 JOHN 10:22		RESTORATION OF TEMPLE IN 164 B.C.
LOTS	PURIM	13-14 ADAR	EST 9	ESTHER	FAILURE OF PLOT AGAINST JEWS BY HAMAN

33. RELIGIOUS GROUPS OUTSIDE JOHN'S COMMUNITY

DIFFERENT RELIGIOUS GROUPINGS OUTSIDE THE JOHANNINE COMMUNITY AS SEEN THROUGH THE PAGES OF THE FOURTH GOSPEL

Those Who Do Not Believe in Jesus			Those Who (Claim To) Believe in Jesus		
I. The World	*II. "The Jews"*	*III. The Adherents of John the Baptist*	*IV. The Crypto-Christians*	*V. The Jewish Christians*	*VI. Christians of Apostolic Churches*
Those who prefer darkness to the light of Jesus because their deeds are evil. By this choice they are already condemned; they are under the power of the Satanic "Prince of this world" and hate Jesus and his disciples who are not of this world. Jesus refuses to pray for the world; rather he has overcome the world. "The world" is a wider conception than "The Jews" (II) but includes them. This opposition gave the Johannine community an alienated sense of being strangers in the world.	Those within the synagogues who did not believe in Jesus and had decided that anybody who acknowledged Jesus as Messiah would be put out of the synagogue. The main points in their dispute with the Johannine Christians involved: (a) Claims about the oneness of Jesus with the Father—the Johannine Jesus "was speaking of God as his own Father, thus making himself God's equal"; (b) Claims that understanding Jesus as God's presence on earth deprived the Temple and the Jewish feasts of their significance. They exposed the Johannine Christians to death by persecution and thought that thus they were serving God. In John's view they were children of the devil.	Although some of JBap's followers joined Jesus or became Christians (including Johannine Christians), others refused, claiming that JBap and not Jesus was God's prime emissary. The Fourth Gospel carefully denies that JBap is the Messiah, Elijah, the Prophet, the light, or the bridegroom. It insists that JBap must decrease while Jesus must increase. Yet the adherents of JBap are pictured as misunderstanding Jesus, not hating him. There seems to remain hope for their conversion.	Christian Jews who had remained within the synagogues by refusing to admit publicly that they believed in Jesus. "They preferred by far the praise of men to the glory of God." Presumably they thought they could retain their private faith in Jesus without breaking from their Jewish heritage. But in the eyes of the Johannine Christians, they thus preferred to be known as disciples of Moses rather than disciples of Jesus. For practical purposes they could be thought of along with "the Jews" (II), although John was implicitly still trying to persuade them to confess their faith publicly.	Christians who had left the synagogues but whose faith in Jesus was inadequate by Johannine standards. They may have regarded themselves as heirs to a Christianity which had existed in Jerusalem under James the brother of the Lord. Presumably their low christology based on miraculous signs was partway between that of Groups IV and VI. They did not accept Jesus' divinity. They did not understand the eucharist as the true flesh and blood of Jesus. In John's view they had ceased to be true believers.	Quite separate from the synagogues, mixed communities of Jews and Gentiles regarded themselves as heirs of the Christianity of Peter and the Twelve. Theirs was a moderately high christology, confessing Jesus as the Messiah born at Bethlehem of Davidic descent and thus Son of God from conception, but without a clear insight into his coming from above in terms of preexistence before creation. In their ecclesiology Jesus may have been seen as the founding father and institutor of the sacraments; but the church now had a life of its own with pastors who carried on apostolic teaching and care. In John's view they did not fully understand Jesus or the teaching function of the Paraclete, but the Johannine Christians prayed for unity with them.

From Raymond Brown, *The Community of the Beloved Disciple* (New York: Paulist, 1979), pp. 168-169.

34. AN OUTLINE OF JOHN'S PASSION

[John 18:1-20:31]

I. THE ARREST AND INTERROGATION OF JESUS
(18:1-27)

A. The Arrest of Jesus (18:1-11)

1.	Setting the scene in the garden	(18:1-3)
2.	Jesus confronts the arresting party	(18:4-8)
3.	Narrator's explanatory addition	(18:10-11)
4.	Peter's response; striking the servant	(18:10-11)

Transition:	Change of scene, Jesus taken from Garden to Annas; Narrator's explanatory addition	(18:12-14)

B. The Interrogation of Jesus (18:14-27)

1.	Entry of Peter and other disciple into High Priest's Palace Peter's first denial	(18:15-18)
2.	Annas interrogates Jesus who protests his innocence	(18:19-23)
3.	Jesus sent to Caiaphas	(18:24)
4.	Peter's second and third denials	(18:25-27)

II. THE TRIAL OF JESUS BEFORE PILATE (18:28–19:16a)

(Outside)	1.	Jewish authorities ask Pilate to condemn Jesus	(18:28-32)
(Inside)	2.	Pilate questions Jesus about kingship	(18:33-38a)
(Outside)	3.	Pilate's first attempt to release Jesus, but "the Jews" prefer Barabbas	(18:28b-40)
(Inside)	4.	Roman soldiers scourge and mock Jesus	(19:1-3)
(Outside)	5.	Pilate presents Jesus to the people, but "the Jews" shout for crucifixion	(19:4-8)
(Inside)	6.	Pilate talks with Jesus about power	(19:9-11)
(Outside)	7.	Pilate gives in to the Jewish demand for Jesus' crucifixion	(19:12-16a)

III. THE EXECUTION OF JESUS ON THE CROSS AND HIS BURIAL (19:16b-42)

1.	Introduction: The way of the cross and the crucifixion	(19:16b-18)
2.	Pilate and the royal inscription	(19:19-22)
3.	The executioners divide Jesus' clothes, the seamless tunic	(19:23-24)
4.	Jesus gives his mother to the Beloved Disciple	(19:25-27)
5.	Jesus thirsts, is given wine, then hands over his spirit	(19:28-30)
6.	The breaking of the legs; the flow of blood and water	(19:31-37)
7.	Conclusion: The burial of Jesus by Joseph and Nicodemus	(19:38-42)

35. THE GOSPEL ACCORDING TO JOHN: OVERVIEW

AUTHORSHIP: Traditionally the evangelist was considered to be John, one of the twelve apostles. Most scholars today do not identify the evangelist as one of the twelve but rather as one who has composed the written gospel using previous traditional sources (e.g. the prologue, a "signs" or miracles source, sayings material, and passion and resurrection narratives) which had been handed down in the community in both oral and written forms from some who had perhaps been eyewitnesses to Jesus.

AUDIENCE: John's community was a mixed group of Jewish and Gentile Christian converts. Many scholars think that the early chapters of the gospel reflect the stages of growth in the community [See # 30 in your SUPPLEMENTARY READINGS]:

1) from an original group of Judean Jews, among whom were followers of John the Baptist, who accepted Jesus as Davidic Messiah,

2) then other Jews who stressed the Mosaic aspect of Jesus and who made converts in Samaria,

3) then Gentiles whose entry would reveal God's plan of fulfillment.

DATE: Most scholars think John's gospel was composed about 90 to 100 A.D. This would place John's gospel about 20 to 30 years after Mark's gospel.

LOCATION: Although there is no absolute certainty, scholars generally agree that John's community was probably located in the area of Ephesus, on the central western coast of Asia Minor.

SITUATION:
The community situation can best be described as one of tension. They are in conflict with their Jewish neighbors who consider them no longer Jews. Apparently by the time the gospel was composed, the Jews had expelled Christians from worship in their synagogues and from their community life. John's gospel reflects the painful divisive situation. Although somewhat embittered by their rejection, John's community now struggles to discover its own Christian identity as no longer Jewish.

They are in tension with their Gentile neighbors because their Christian life and practices are different. But their Christian identity must be developed amidst the pluralism of the Hellenistic culture, whose practices and religious outlook have not yet been influenced by Christianity at all.

And, finally, to a certain extent, they are in tension with other Christian communities over issues of theology (e.g. Christ as pre-existent or an idea of the end-time as "realized" already with the coming of the Holy Spirit) and community organization (e.g. a less hierarchical and more egalitarian understanding of Church).

PURPOSE:
The gospel is meant to strengthen the faith of the Christian community as it tries to live out its commitment to Christ amidst the various tensions with which it lives. John 20:31 expresses this purpose quite clearly: "But these [signs] are written that you may [come to] believe that Jesus is the Messiah, the Son of God, and that through this belief you may have life in his name." Reading this gospel teaches us to "see" beyond the "signs," and discover Jesus as God's unique revelation of "the way, the truth, and the life" (14:6).

CHARACTERISTICS AND STYLE:
John's style is dramatic, repetitive, and characterized by such stylistic devices as inclusion, chiasm (inverted parallelism), irony, i.e. twofold or double meaning, and explanatory notes from the editor. He prefers to involve Jesus in dialogues with other characters which then introduce long monologues in which Jesus clarifies the truths of his message from God.

JOHANNINE THEMES:

Some of the major themes in John's gospel are:

faith

signs

life

light

love

sin

glory (of God)

God as Father

Jesus as Son sent

Holy Spirit/Paraclete

discipleship

   (note "the disciple whom Jesus loves")

Baptism

Eucharist

revelation

works

word

sight/blindness

above/below

"the Jews"

"the world"

JOHN'S PORTRAIT OF JESUS:

As the pre-existent Word of God, Jesus is the true revealer of God's divine self. He is with God and is God and the agent of all that is created. He can claim the divine name "I AM." As the Son of God who has been sent into our world for salvation, Jesus is the Messiah. He is also the Son of Man who comes down from above to suffer, be glorified, and return to the Father. He replaces the Jewish feasts with himself and fulfills the religious longings of all humanity.

Although the pre-existent Son of the Father, Jesus takes on "flesh," i.e. becomes genuinely human. He speaks what he hears the Father saying and does what the Father sent him to do. This speaking and doing invites persons to believe in him and so to eternal life. He can do this because he and the Father are one — sharing divinity and life which in turn are shared with those who believe.

JOHN'S PORTRAIT OF DISCIPLESHIP:

A disciple is one who comes to see where the Lord dwells and dwells with him, who invites the Lord to dwell with him or her. The main sign of discipleship is an intimate, loving relationship with Jesus and hence with the Father and the Paraclete. Disciples are called to love one another as Jesus has loved them.

The ideal is set forth through the character of the Beloved Disciple who:

— is intimate with Jesus

— really understands Jesus because of the love they share

— "sees" and "believes" when others do not yet do so

— follows Jesus to the cross and at the word of Jesus forms with his Mother the genuine faith community after the death of Jesus

— recognizes the risen "glorified" Lord present in their midst

THE GOSPEL PATTERN:

Chapters 1 – 12: THE BOOK OF SIGNS

A narration of the words and deeds of Jesus as "signs" which invite a faith response. Jesus' presence in our world — "the Son sent for salvation" — is also a judgment.

Chapters 13 – 21: THE BOOK OF GLORY

A narration of Jesus' return to the Father and so to his glorification. This is achieved through his "passover" of death/resurrection and his sending of the Paraclete to complete his work through the community of disciples.

36. APOCALYPTIC LITERATURE: OVERVIEW

"Apocalyptic" comes from the Greek word meaning to reveal, to take the veil off. It claims to see and understand the hidden perspective of God for our world. So writing identified this way claims to offer a privileged understanding of the secrets of heaven and earth and the secrets of the future course of our world. This occurs through a message which has been given to the author through some special form, e.g. visions, oracles, otherworldly journeys, or access to heavenly books.

Historically, this type of literature arises in response to a religious community's dissatisfaction with the views and claims of their surrounding culture. The community's crisis involves a discrepancy between their political and economic situation and the promises of their religious heritage. Hence, Walter Brueggemann describes apocalyptic literature as "the visionary rage of those victimized by the present order" (*The Land*, p. 163). This style of writing was particularly prevalent during the later post-exilic life of Israel under the Hellenistic Selucid Dynasty and the first two centuries of Christianity (c. 200 B.C. to 200 A.D.).

Apocalyptic is an expression of a community's faith that God is present in our world to save us because God loves us. In examining their situation through "eyes of faith," the community seeks to discern

1. Where is God to save us?
2. How will God do it?
3. What ought we to do?

Clues about the answers to these questions are embedded in the past history and the sacred texts of the community. Although different in style, this type of writing presents an understanding of God that depends very much on images, symbols, and stories already familiar to the audience. (For example, over half of the verses in the NT Book of Revelation contain either direct quotes or allusions to the Old Testament!)

WHY APOCALYPTIC IS WRITTEN

Apocalyptic literature answers the need for an alternative vision of reality, one which includes God's presence, reverses the fortunes of the persecuted community, and transforms the present reality into a shape that can only now be imagined.

The aim of the author is:

1) to strengthen the faith (= trust) of God's people under trial in anticipation of the final and decisive intervention of God into our world for salvation. This will mark the end of history as we know it and will bring in the rule of God over all the world.

2) to provide consolation and hope by recognizing not only God's sovereignty but also God's judgment of the evil powers of the world which now persecute the community. Not only will God rule, but God will punish those who now persecute the community.

The viewpoint or perspective of the author is a double vision. The author sees clearly the pain and suffering involved in living out one's religious commitment in a hostile world, but, more importantly, the author sees and evaluates this experience from God's viewpoint. God's presence in power for salvation will master the powers of evil at work in our world. The apocalyptic vision both unveils God's perspective on our sinful world and imaginatively portrays the coming triumph of God over evil and the consequent punishment of evildoers and persecutors. When the dust of this cosmic struggle clears, the author envisions a new relationship of our world to God.

THE LITERARY STYLE OF APOCALYPTIC

Apocalyptic literature is a dramatic, visionary presentation of God's presence in our world for salvation and judgment. Since it does not present reality simply as it is, but primarily as it is meant to be when God rules, apocalyptic literature is highly imaginative. It takes us into a strange world where the ordinary rules of reality no longer prevail. Because of its dependence upon the imagination of the author and of the reader who is to understand it, this literature is characterized by:

1) symbolism —
   code words which stand for other realities (not just pictures of these realities), e.g. names, numbers, animals, colors, scenes, nature, etc.
2) pseudonymous authorship —
   attributed to historical figures, e.g. Daniel, Moses (The Book of Revelation seems to be an exception to this general rule.)
3) two-story (or three-story) universe Heaven / earth / (hell)
4) dramatic struggle of good/evil for decisive control of the earth
5) extensive activity attributed to more-than-human beings (angels/demons)
6) imaginative descriptions of cosmic catastrophes
7) coded presentation of historical events

TIPS FOR READING AND INTERPRETING APOCALYPTIC

Many readers have great difficulty with apocalyptic because of its obscure imagery and its fanatical tendencies. But "the key to a proper appreciation of the apocalyptic tradition lies in the realization that apocalypses are more of the nature of poetry than of dogma. They are works of the imagination, which cannot be regarded as sources of factual information. Their value lies in their ability to envision alternatives to the world of present experience and thereby to provide hope and consolation." (John J. Collins, "Old Testament Apocalypticism and Eschatology," *The New Jerome Biblical Commentary*, p. 304.)

As we read this literature, then, we must be prepared

- to use our imagination to picture a world which transcends our everyday world
- to be ready for the reversal of ordinary reality
- to have our normal perceptions and expectations challenged by the strange new world that is presented in the text
- to look not for a smooth flow of the narrative but rather for a disjointed series of diverse units whose logic is more like that of a dream than a dogmatic treatise
- to let the associative power of the symbols provide a new insight into the meaning of the historical events of our world
- to heed the announcement of the end of things as they are and the opening up of the reality of things as God wants them to be

As always with the interpretation of texts, we must work hard to discover:

1) what this text *MEANT* to the author and the original readers in their own situation.

2) what this text *MEANS* for us who consider it inspired revelation, and thus somehow normative for our own understanding of who God is and what it means to be Christian today.

37. UNDERSTANDING THE BOOK OF REVELATION

By Macrina Scott, O.S.F.

The Book of Revelation is the last book in the Bible, and probably also the strangest. Opening it at random, you may feel as if you have stumbled into a child's nightmare: "Then I saw a wild beast come out of the sea with ten horns and seven heads; on its horns were ten diadems and on its heads blasphemous names. The beast I saw was like a leopard, but it had paws like a bear and the mouth of a lion" (Revelation 13:1-2).

One such picture follows another in bewildering profusion. It is no wonder that throughout the history of the Church, Christians have searched for a key with which they could unlock some meaning in this bizarre world of visions. Often some contemporary political event seems to fit: the ravages of Attila the Hun, the rise of Hitler, some catastrophic earthquake. Today people are likely to use Stalin, Castro or a U.S. president as keys for unraveling the meaning. We can be sure that, whatever happens on the world scene in generations to come, someone will find it predicted in the Book of Revelation.

Today biblical scholarship has tools with which to study Revelation more objectively. Scholars are now able to compare it with other books written in the same literary style at the same period. They have painstakingly unraveled the complex pattern in which it is composed and studied the background of each symbol used. After many years of research, they have discovered the key, which was so well hidden it had been overlooked by innumerable readers — the first three chapters of the book itself! There the author states fairly clearly what he will develop again and again in elaborate symbolic language throughout the remainder of the book. We can find the answers to our main questions about Revelation in those three chapters.

Who Wrote It?

One thing we instinctively want to know about any book is who wrote it. We want to know the name of the author. More important, we want to know where the author is coming from, what life experiences have determined the author's point of view and colored his or her vision of the world. The author gives us his name in the first chapter of Revelation: John — a common name which probably identified him for his first readers but is not much help to us nineteen centuries later. Some readers have thought he is John the Apostle, but he says nothing to indicate that. Some think he is the author of John's Gospel, but he does not say that either, and it is hard to imagine that one person could write two books so different in style.

What *is* clear, and very helpful in understanding the book, is that he tells us where he is coming from: "I, John, your brother...found myself on the island called Patmos because I proclaimed God's word and bore witness to Jesus" (Revelation 1:9). John is a man deeply conscious of belonging to the Christian community, suffering an enforced separation from his brothers and sisters. He has been sentenced to the penal colony on the rocky little island of Patmos because of his witness to Jesus.

As we see in other parts of the New Testament, the early Christians were law-abiding citizens who appreciated the benefits of civil government and tried to live on peaceful terms with the Roman authorities who controlled their world (see Romans 13:1-7; 1 Peter 2:13-17). John may at one time have shared that point of view. But the situation was changing. He probably wrote during the reign of Emperor Domitian, 81 to 96 A.D. Domitian enforced the demand that citizens of the empire not only obey his laws and pay his taxes, but also worship him. He even demanded to be addressed as "Lord and God."

It was not a simple issue, and not all Christians agreed on the proper response. A statue of the emperor was set up in a public place, and loyal citizens were expected to prostrate themselves before it. (The Greek word for this action is often translated into English as "worship." It recurs throughout Revelation: People worship or prostrate themselves either before God or before the Beast.) Few, if any, of the early Christians' pagan neighbors actually thought the emperor was God. The gesture meant little more to them than saluting the flag means to an American. It was an expression of patriotic enthusiasm and loyalty to a political leader.

The Jews, on the other hand, saw the gesture and the offering of incense that went with it as honor that belonged to God alone. They proved so stubborn on the matter that the emperors found it prudent to grant them a special exemption. The very first Christians had been considered a branch of the Jewish community, so they shared the exemption granted the Jews. But John was writing after the Christians had been expelled from the synagogue. They had to face increasingly strong demands for emperor worship just at the time when they had lost the protection of the exemption granted the Jews.

New and difficult questions of conscience arose. The Roman government was in general a good thing; the early Christians were not revolutionaries. But at this point, thought some Christians, it had overstepped the boundaries of what a government had a right to demand and had set itself up as a rival to God. If these radical Christians refused to pay the customary marks of reverence to the emperor, they were liable to be martyred or sent, like John, to the bleak island of Patmos. If they refused to use the coins marked with the image of the "divine emperor," they would be unable to buy or sell, and economic ruin would be inevitable (see Revelation 13:15-17). Many felt the path of compromise was the wiser one.

Christians today can understand the anguished soul-searching of these early Christians by listening to the questions that surround the nuclear armaments issue. If it is immoral to build up stockpiles of nuclear weapons for the demolition of the human race and the environment, what respect can a Christian pay to a government that is doing just that? Has it gone beyond the boundaries of the loyalty appropriate to it as a civil government into opposing the Lord of life? If so, what is the obligation of the Christian? Can she or he salute the flag which represents this government? Is it moral to pay taxes that will be used to manufacture nuclear weapons? The new reality of nuclear armaments creates new and complex questions, and Christians do not agree about the answers.

New laws enforcing emperor worship, plus separation from the protection of the synagogue, created a new situation for the Christians to whom John wrote. John himself had come to see total resistance to the Roman Empire as his duty to God. He believed that one must choose between worshiping the emperor and worshiping God. Out of this deep conviction he had performed some action that resulted in his banishment to Patmos. There, in the long lonely hours, he prayed, and his convictions deepened.

One Sunday as his fellow Christians across the sea were gathering for the Eucharist, John gazed toward the shore of Asia Minor where they lived and received a vision he felt would inspire these much-loved sisters and brothers to share his attitude of resistance to the mighty Roman Empire.

To Whom Is It Written?

John wrote to seven churches of Asia Minor (modern Turkey), forty miles across the Mediterranean from Patmos. He knew these communities well, and described their spiritual condition in detail.

Many modern readers find that the seven churches also represent various stages of faithfulness and unfaithfulness into which the church or the individual Christian is liable to fit at any period. One way of praying over these chapters is to look for the church which seems most like your own spiritual condition, and listen to the message of the Spirit for that church as a message for yourself.

What Did John See?

As John sat on his lonely island, thinking of the Christians he loved so much, he saw a symbolic vision: "I saw seven lampstands of gold, and among the lampstands One like a Son of Man wearing an ankle-length robe, with a sash of gold about his breast. The hair of his head was as white as snow-white wool and his eyes blazed like fire. His feet gleamed like polished brass refined in a furnace, and his voice sounded like the roar of rushing waters. In his right hand he held seven stars. A sharp, two-edged sword came out of his mouth, and his face shone like the sun at its brightest" (Revelation 1:12-15).

The lampstands, he was soon told, were the seven churches. The wonderful figure who walked among them like a shepherd among his sheep was Jesus, the risen Lord. Like all the visions that will follow, this one is meant to evoke a general impression, not to draw a detailed picture. A literalist might wonder how Jesus talked if he was holding a two-edged sword in his mouth, but John does not expect us to read in that way. He wants to give us a feeling of the *power* of the risen Lord and to reassure us that this figure, stronger even than the emperor, walks among the churches and strengthens them by his presence.

The vision of the risen Christ is central to the entire book, which explains why the Church has traditionally read the Book of Revelation during Eastertide. In the vision Jesus identifies himself significantly as "the One who lives. Once I was dead but now I live — forever and ever" (Revelation 1:18). John is eager to show the Christians, whom

he expects to be called to martyrdom, that Jesus had also passed through martyrdom to the Resurrection, and that the overwhelming power of the emperor pales into insignificance beside the power Jesus has. He speaks of "Jesus Christ the faithful witness (the word for "witness" is the same as that for "martyr" in the original Greek), the first-born from the dead and the ruler of the kings of the earth" (Revelation 1:5).

The Reading for All Saints

…After this I saw before me a huge crowd which no one could count from every nation, race, people, and tongue. They stood before the throne and the Lamb, dressed in long, white robes and holding palm branches in their hands. They cried out in a loud voice: "Salvation is from our God, who is seated on the throne; and from the Lamb!" All the angels who were standing around the throne and the elders and the four living creatures fell down before the throne to worship God. They said: "Amen! Praise and glory, wisdom, thanksgiving, and honor, power and might, to our God forever and ever. Amen!"

Then one of the elders asked me, "Who do you think these are, all dressed in white? And where have they come from?" I said to him, "Sir, you should know better than I." He then told me, "These are the ones who have survived the great period of trial; they have washed their robes and made them white in the blood of the Lamb."

Revelation 7:9–14

John does not see the Resurrection of Christ merely as something that happened in the past. Christ is the "first-born from the dead," a sign of the death and glory that await everyone who is faithful to him. Especially in the last two chapters of Revelation, John will expand his vision to the entire universe, which will pass through a death experience before the whole of it is glorified and taken up into God's presence as Jesus was.

What Is the Point?

The message which the risen Christ sends to the seven churches through John is a series of cosmic panoramas, like some tremendous multimedia presentation of an ultimate struggle between the forces of good and the forces of evil. John is thinking of the coming persecution of Christian communities by Roman power, but he wants to show the ordinary little people who compose these communities that they are part of a battle far greater than this world. Though they may die what the world sees as a shameful death, in reality they will be the victors, heroes in the army of the victorious Christ, who has already overcome death in his own resurrection and will complete the conquest at his second coming.

The message is first a warning, trying to shake the Christians loose from complacency, call them away from compromise with secular powers and warn them of the approaching crisis. "Repent. If you do not rouse yourselves I will come upon you like a thief, at a time you cannot know" (Revelation 3:3). John deliberately stirs his readers to fear by his warnings. He paints a vivid symbolic picture of all the horrors which the Beast will accomplish. Then he shows a vision of the victory which does not *replace* death and disaster, but *follows* them. He adds a new dimension that gives the suffering meaning without removing it.

The advice John gives again and again is, "Hold fast, remain faithful, endure." It is a message of nonviolent resistance to an evil government. There is no suggestion that the tiny Christian community should attempt to overthrow the government or change its policies. The power of God will overcome the powers of evil. The individual person is not shown as directly influencing the outcome, but as deciding on which side of the struggle to stand, whether to worship the Beast (the Roman Empire) or God. The faithful Christian is one who chooses to worship God at any cost.

Why Does It Sound So Strange?

It does not surprise us that John, already in prison for his faith, should write to his fellow Christians to warn them of a coming large-scale persecution and to encourage them to hope and persevere. But why did John need such a strange conglomeration of blood and fire, beasts, battles and plagues, angels, trumpets and heavenly beings to communicate his message?

He was using the literary style called *apocalyptic*, which was familiar to his first-century readers. Many of the symbols had commonly accepted meanings. Seven and twelve were numbers representing totality; three and a half, six and 666 represented imperfection. Thrones and crowns were symbolic of power. Clouds, rainbows, thunder and lightning were signs of the divine presence. However, the work is much more than an encoded message calling on the reader for a little intellectual effort to reduce it to ordinary language. Its images are more like those of dreams, vivid and meaningful, but incapable of being totally contained in conceptual language.

John composed this dramatic work to be read aloud at Christian worship. Perhaps the best way to hear his message is to relax, lay aside efforts at logic and simply absorb the imagery and sound, movement and color of the work. We would probably experience more of what John intended if we had the opportunity to attend a multimedia presentation of Revelation.

For a more detailed understanding of the entire work, a commentary is essential. Two fine popular commentaries are *The Apocalypse*, by Adela Yarbro Collins, and *Invitation to the Book of Revelation*, by Elisabeth Schussler Fiorenza. These contain the information gathered by students of apocalyptic literature to make sense of the details of the visions.

The reader who does not want to spend time unraveling all the details with the help of a commentary can still benefit spiritually from meditating on the first three chapters, and also on the beautiful visions of heaven in chapters 4, 5, 21 and 22. Anyone with a sense for poetic imagery can feel in these chapters John's message of hope, based on his conviction that there is a spiritual world more real than the world we see, and that one day it will triumph completely over all the evils we experience in this world.

What Does It Have To Say Today?

Why should Americans of the 20th century read a message intended to prepare Christians of the first century for the persecution of Domitian?

The feeling of many individuals today as they face inflation, the breakdown of family life and the nuclear threat is a feeling of powerlessness. One who feels powerless is tempted to despair, not motivated to stand against the dominant culture. John is writing to a tiny Christian minority, composed mostly of the lower classes, who also felt powerless against the dominant structure of their world, the Roman Empire. He promises that the Christian who is a faithful witness until death will share in Christ's victory against all the powers of evil. He tells the powerless and oppressed of the 20th century as well as the first that their choices are important.

John's heroes, those who follow Christ in the fullest way, are the martyrs. (Elisabeth Schussler Fiorenza accordingly dedicates her commentary on the Book of Revelation to Archbishop Oscar Romero and other Christians of our times who have been killed for their resistance to unjust governments.) In the honor they paid to the martyrs, the Christians of John's time became vividly aware of the communion of saints, the bonds of mutual concern and shared worship of God that bind together Christians on earth and their sisters and brothers who have died. We can see why the

Church has always used the Book of Revelation in the celebration of All Saints Day.

Those in our own country and throughout the world who are imprisoned for reasons of conscience, jailed because they refuse to allow obedience to the state to take precedence over obedience to God, should be particularly encouraged by this book written by John in just such a situation.

Those of us who are tempted to compromise with whatever powers of evil try to control our lives can learn from the warnings in the first chapters against such compromise. It is for our benefit particularly that John gives such vivid symbolic pictures of the powers of evil. We would like to make peace with the powers that surround us, and yet continue to worship God. We see the world more in shades of gray than in black and white. There are parts of the Bible that support such attitudes, but Revelation is not one of them. It is a book for those times in our personal lives or in the life of the Church when the grays fall away and we are forced to take a stand in the great struggle between the forces of good and the forces of evil. At such times, Christians are grateful for the mind-stretching visions of the prisoner of Patmos.

38. THE BOOK OF REVELATION: OVERVIEW

DATE: 90 - 100 A.D. (most likely about 95)

LOCATION: John is writing from exile on the island of Patmos, some 30-40 miles off shore from the mainland of Asia Minor, in the Aegean Sea. He is writing to seven churches in Asia Minor, moving in a clockwise direction from Ephesus.

SITUATION: Christian communities in Asia Minor perceive their situation to be one of crisis. They feel alienated and perhaps are afraid of being singled out for persecution by the powerful Roman Empire, most probably near the end of the reign of Emperor Domitian (81-96).

Apparently there was an enforcement of the demand not only to pay taxes, obey the civil laws, etc. but also to worship the emperor as divine. Although Jews were exempt from this worship, Christians were not because the Romans no longer considered Christians to be Jews. This situation posed new and difficult questions of conscience for the Christian communities. John sees his duty to God as uncompromising and passes this message on to his fellow Christians.

PURPOSE: By using the visionary style of apocalyptic literature, John hopes to give his communities a new perspective on how God is present in their situation. Hope for the future is elicited by giving the community a deeper understanding of how God, who had been active in their past from creation until now, is still at work now to bring salvation and judgment in their present need.

The book is written to call Christians to shake loose from any complacency or compromise with secular powers and to encourage them during their crisis. The author paints a vivid picture of the victory which is theirs in Christ. Although the community is assured that God's victory will certainly occur, this knowledge does not automatically free them from their present suffering.

AUTHOR:

The exact identity of the author is impossible to determine. The text tells us that:

— The author was a Christian named John, who had been banished for a time to the Island of Patmos as punishment for his Christian allegiance and witness.

— He had connection and influence among the seven churches of Asia which he expects to heed his warnings and attend to his message.

— He claims to be a brother of his readers and a partner in their sufferings. He speaks to them in familiar terms.

— He is a person claiming prophetic and visionary gifts and is led by God to write a message for the churches of Asia Minor.

Although a long tradition identifies this John with John the Apostle and son of Zebedee, most scholars do not identify the two. Eusebius (Bishop of Caesarea), in his *History of the Church*, quotes the early second century witness Papias who distinguished between John the Apostle and John the Elder.

Furthermore, scholars do not identify the author of Revelation with the author of the gospel of John. This view can be found as early as the third century, e.g by Dionysius, a Bishop of Alexandria, who claimed that the gospel, the letters and Revelation could not possibly come from the same author.

AUDIENCE: The circular letters indicate that the message is for the Christian communities located in seven cities of Asia Minor: Ephesus, Smyrna, Pergamum, Thyatira, Sardis, Philadelphia, and Laodicea.

STYLE: The author employs the visionary style of apocalyptic writing (see # 36, p. 142 in your SUPPLEMENTARY READINGS). By recalling their past dealings with God (there are about 500 allusions to the Old Testament in Revelation), the author wants to inspire hope for God's saving presence in the midst of their current suffering.

MAJOR THEMES:

— God's presence in power in our world (Lordship, Kingdom)

— God's salvation for the faithful

— God's judgment for the wicked

— God's utter transcendence (almighty, holy, Creator)

— Paradox of God's power and love in action

— Christ's oneness with God (Lord of Lords, King of Kings)

— Christ's oneness with the Church

— God's victory over evil

— Dualisms: heaven/earth, good/evil

— Church/state relations

— Mediated revelation

— Continuity of Salvation History to the present time

— Incomplete character of God's redemptive work

— Christian hope in time of suffering

— Exhortation to "hold fast"; "remain faithful"; "turn to God"; "endure"

PORTRAIT OF GOD: Father, Alpha and Omega, The Almighty, Judge of all creation, Ultimate Ruler of all; One to be worshipped, Creator of all, Source of all life.

PORTRAIT OF JESUS:

Faithful witness

Firstborn from the dead

Ruler of Kings of the earth (Lord of Lords and King of Kings)

The Lamb that was slain

Opener of the mysteries of life and death, Salvation History

Judge of all creation

Lover who freed us from our sins and made us a royal nation of priests in serving the Father

Plus many symbolic associations made in John's visions, e.g. Alpha and Omega, powerful, dead now alive, tongue as two-edged sword, eyes like fire, feet like brass, holding the seven stars, holy and true, holding the key of David, the "Amen," the true and faithful witness.

PORTRAIT OF DISCIPLESHIP:

Genuine disciples are those who:

— remain faithful, endure, hope, and worship God no matter what the cost

— turn from complacency and compromise and trust God alone to help them

39. SELF-QUIZ: THE GOSPEL OF JOHN AND REVELATION

THE GOSPEL OF JOHN

1.   WHEN was the Gospel of John written?

2.   WHO was John's original audience?

3.   WHERE was this audience probably located?

4.   WHAT was the situation in which John's community found themselves?

5.   WHAT was the evangelist's original purpose in writing this book?

6.   What do you consider to be the TWO most important themes in this book?

    1.

    2.

7.   How would you characterize the portrait of Jesus in John?

8.   How would you describe John's understanding of "genuine discipleship"?

9.   What is the most significant thing you have learned from this book?

10. Be able to locate the following on a map of the Holy Land:
     Cana, Bethany, Bethsaida, Sychar, Capernaum, Judea, Samaria, Galilee, Dead Sea, and the
     Sea of Galilee (Sea of Tiberias in John)

DEFINITIONS: Briefly but accurately identify the following:

1)   "High" Christology
2)   "Paraclete"
3)   "The Beloved Disciple"

REVELATION

1. WHEN was the Book of Revelation written?

2. WHO was the original audience?

3. WHERE was this audience located?

4. WHAT was the author's original purpose in writing this book?

5. What do you consider to be the TWO most important themes in this book?

    1.

    2.

6. How would you describe the portrait of Jesus in this book?

7. How would you describe "genuine discipleship" in this book?

8. What is the most significant thing you have learned from this book?

9. Briefly define the meaning of "apocalyptic literature."

10. Be able to locate the seven churches of the Book of Revelation and Patmos.

40. Map Quizzes

1. Place the following where they
belong on the map:

Cana

Bethany

Bethsaida

Sychar

Capernaum

Judea

Samaria

Galilee

Dead Sea

Sea of Tiberias

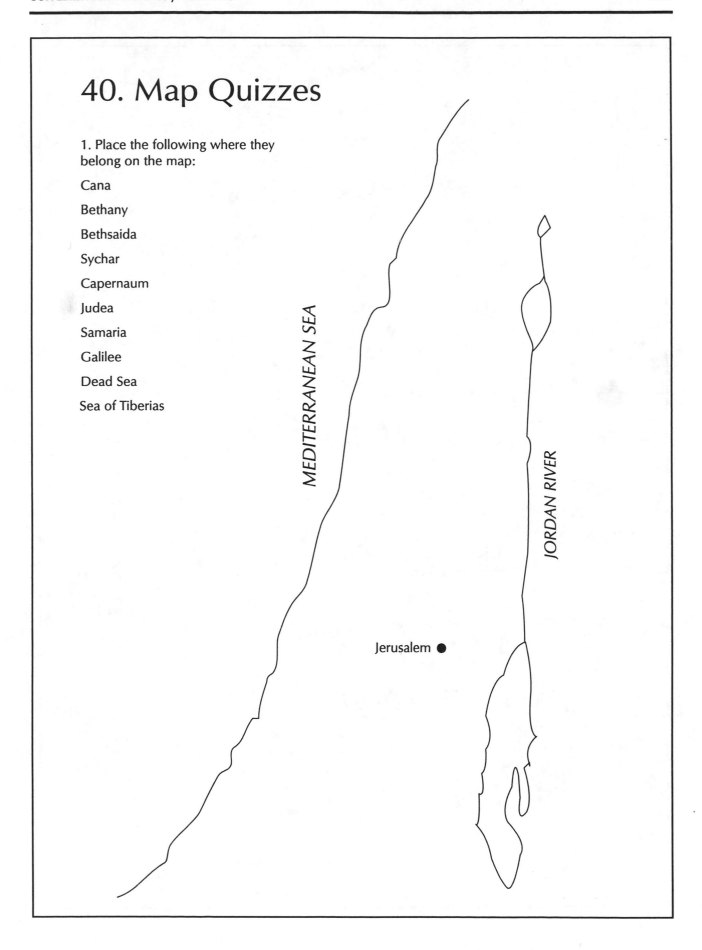

MEDITERRANEAN SEA

JORDAN RIVER

Jerusalem ●

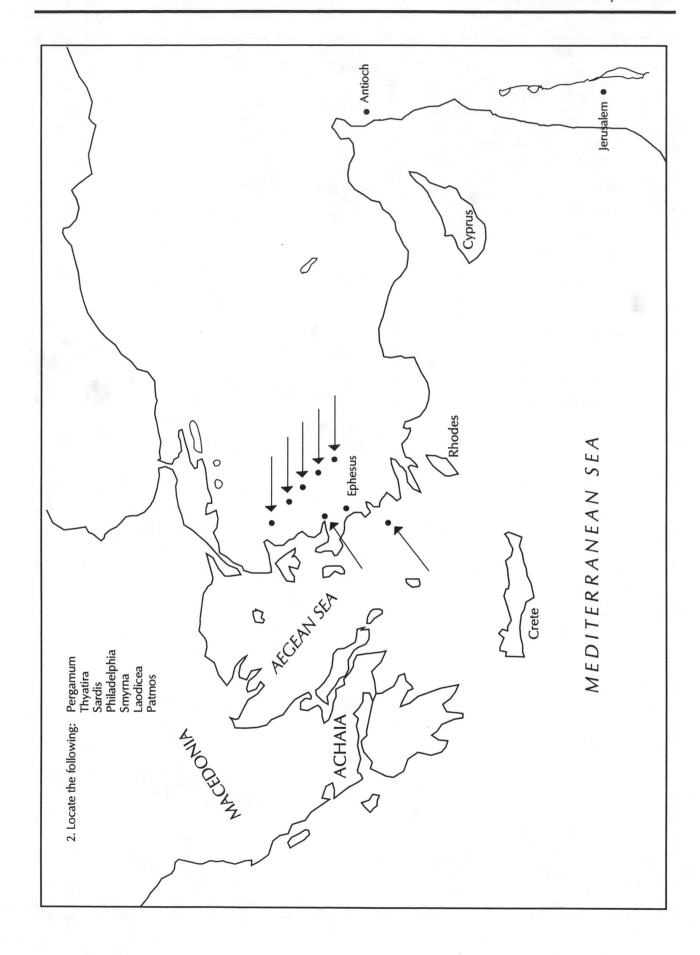

2. Locate the following: Pergamum
                           Thyatira
                           Sardis
                           Philadelphia
                           Smyrna
                           Laodicea
                           Patmos

MACEDONIA

ACHAIA

AEGEAN SEA

MEDITERRANEAN SEA

Crete

Rhodes

Cyprus

Ephesus

Antioch

Jerusalem